THE RATIONAL FAITH

THE
RATIONAL FAITH

A Systematic Exposition of Catholic Doctrine

MATTHEW I. GRIVICH, PH.D.

SAN DIEGO PRESS   SAN DIEGO, CA

NIHIL OBSTAT
I have concluded that the materials presented in this work are free of doctrinal or moral errors.
Bernadeane M. Carr, STL
May 24th, 2011

IMPRIMATUR
In accord with 1983 CIC 827 § 3, permission to publish this work is hereby granted.
+ Robert H. Brom
Bishop of San Diego
May 24th, 2011

Printed in the United States of America.

ISBN 978-0-9837121-0-7

Cover design by Matthew Grivich. Image shown is of Holy Cross Church, in Santa Cruz, CA.

Contents

CHAPTER 1:
Introduction

A voice cries out:
In the desert prepare the way of the LORD!
(Isaiah 40:3)

1.1 Purpose

The goal of this book is to put Christianity on a firm
intellectual footing. Assuming this is not the first place you
have looked, you have learned that there is a large amount of
nonsense written both for and against Christianity and that it
is easy to despair of ever finding a reliable source. Even when
you find well-thought-out sources, every proof and opinion is
based on assumptions that have not been substantiated. You
can read an entire book and never feel confident that the earliest
foundations of the author's arguments were well-established.
It is my desire to help improve this situation. As you read this
book, you will find the discussion organized in such a way
that you can see every logical dependency at a glance. It is my
hope to use this device to prove Christianity to you beyond a
reasonable doubt. There are few, if any, genuinely new ideas in
this book. However, with this device you can understand the
rational core of the faith much more rapidly than if you had to
read and organize the thousands of pages that I used as source
material.

This book is targeted at those who have some sympathy for the Christian world view, but find their intellect getting in the way. You may be a practicing Christian, but selective in what part of the faith you practice. You may be an atheist who is unsatisfied with the problematic conclusions of atheism. You may be a devout Christian, but wish your faith had more foundation. You may be spiritual, but not Christian, and wishing to expand your understanding of the Christian faith. This book works to resolve intellectual challenges by feeding the intellect with the nutrients that it requires. If you have no primitive sympathy for the Christian world view, then no argument, no matter how rational or factual, will convince you.

You must be willing to question your long held assumptions and resolve to question my argumentation. This book will only be valuable to you if you have a genuine desire to learn. Even if you learn something other than what I intend to teach, aspire to make your time with this book as valuable to you as possible. In this way, your time (and mine) will not be wasted.

I should also say what this book is not. It is not a balanced survey of current thought on Christianity. It is a balanced survey of *my* thoughts on Christianity. I will bring up opposing arguments sometimes, but only to counter-argue. My views are those of orthodox Catholic Christianity, and I do not knowingly contradict the Church in this book.

1.2 Fundamental Assumptions

I say above that I desire not merely to explain my beliefs about Christianity, but to prove them to you. Ideally, this means that I make zero assumptions. In practice, this is not possible. There are two assumptions that are, by their very nature, not provable. I can make them plausible, but I cannot prove them. However, realize that rejecting these assumptions means rejecting all human knowledge, not just philosophy or theology.

1.2.1 Truth Is Logically Consistent

That is, the statements:

1) A equals B
2) A does not equal B,

cannot both be true. Other statements, such as A cannot be both greater and less than B fall under the same category. All proofs depend upon this assumption. You cannot prove that truth is logically consistent, because all proofs require the consistency of logic as an assumption. However, the premise is a reasonable one. All of current science and engineering depends upon it. A computer follows the laws of logic. If it did not, it would be impossible to design one that functioned. The ideal laws of science are self-consistent. In the past, whenever a law of science has been inconsistent with another law, the problem has been with the laws, not with the universe. In the present era, one of the primary motivations behind theoretical physics is contradiction removal, because it has been so useful in the past. It would be strange indeed if everything in the physical universe is self-consistent; but once you start asking questions about the deeper nature of reality consistency is broken.

1.2.2 Language Has Meaning

That is, this book reveals actual concepts that you are capable of understanding, in the same way that I understand them. I must be careful to define unusual or difficult concepts; but once this is done, it is possible for me to relay information to you. It is impossible to prove that language has meaning, because no proof can be made without language. This premise is plausible, because all of science and engineering depends upon this, as well as all human relationships. I would not be able to repeat experiments carried out by Isaac Newton and get the same answers unless we had a shared understanding of what he wrote in the *Principia,* more than three hundred years ago. Language, however, can be an issue in any conversation. It is important when you read this book, that you use my vocabulary. For example, I speak of God frequently. In the beginning, my understanding, and therefore my definition, of God is very minimalist. As we learn more about God, I expand my definition, until it matches that of the Christian God. It is important that you follow these changing definitions in order to properly understand my book.

In addition, there are also a number of facts that I assume because I believe that every rational and educated person accepts them. This includes basic things, such as the knowledge that a hydrogen atom is composed of a proton and an electron, as well as more advanced things, such as the understanding that humans are conscious.

1.3 Faith and Reason

As discussed in the previous section, we must be careful to agree on the meaning of the words we use. One such word is "faith." It is used in many different and not entirely consistent ways. Usually which definition is being used must be determined from context.

Blind faith is to believe something to be true without adequate evidence. When atheists say faith, this is frequently what they mean. I will never use the word in this way, as I am incapable of discovering truth through blind faith.

Faithfulness is to be loyal to an idea, a person, or God. This is not a matter of belief, but a matter of commitment, as a wife is faithful to her husband, and a husband is faithful to his wife. This type of faith is important, but is not the focus of this book.

Personal faith, as the term is used by Catholic theologians, is a free assent of a person to the whole truth that God has revealed in scripture. I occasionally use the word in this way.

Personal faith, as the term is used by non-Catholics, is typically a belief system of a particular person. What it depends on (scripture, experience, etcetera) depends on the person. I will not use the term this way in this book.

The Catholic faith is the collection of truths promulgated by the Catholic Church and summarized in the Apostles' and Nicene Creeds. This is the meaning of faith that I use in the phrase, "the rational faith." When I speak of faith in this book, this is usually the kind of faith I am talking about.

A faith tradition is a collection of fundamental beliefs accepted to be true by a group of people or an organization. This is similar to the previous definition for faith, except that it does not explicitly refer to Catholic teaching. When I use this term, I am explicit in writing "faith tradition."

I must also discuss different types of reasoning. In practical as well as technical discussions, they often blur together.

Inductive (a posteriori) reasoning is extrapolating and generalizing from experience to gain knowledge. This is the most basic form of knowledge as even young children are capable of it. It is always limited by our ability to experience all relevant situations necessary to form a proper conclusion.

Deductive (a priori) reasoning is deriving conclusions from premises by following the rules of logic. Premises cannot come from deductive reasoning, so deductive reasoning can never be confirmed to correspond to truth without some inductive reasoning.

Scientific reasoning is using the scientific method to gain knowledge. Science uses both inductive (experimental) and deductive (theoretical) reasoning with the added principle that experiment and theory inform and correct each other explicitly.

Biblical reasoning uses both inductive and deductive reasoning, with the legitimacy of the Bible accepted as a premise. Inductive biblical reasoning consists largely of reading scripture directly to determine truth. Deductive biblical reasoning takes what was learned while reading scripture and derives appropriate conclusions.

In Catholic theology, it is standard to speak of knowledge gained through philosophy and science as reason-based while speaking of knowledge gained through scripture as faith-based. However, the language is difficult, because theologians still use inductive and deductive reasoning when studying scripture. The difference is that instead of using the natural world or ordinary experience as their data, they use scripture. Before this can be done, the authority of scripture must be justified. In this book, I speak of rational proofs which find their source data in science, philosophy, or scripture. I do not typically explicitly categorize these as faith- or reason-based, but it easy to tell by noting the nature of the source data.

1.4 Outline

I will begin with a discussion of arguments against Christianity (Chapter 2). The purpose here is to remove specific objections that you may have early, so that we may start with as blank of a slate as possible. We must have a blank slate before we can build a solid foundation. The foundation is that of philosophy. There are two main goals here (Chapter 3). The first is to make it acceptable to believe by showing, through example, how consistent science is with the Christian faith. The second goal is to actively build a proto-Christian philosophy without referring to scripture. I will do this both because I can, and because then the teachings of scripture will be comfortable and familiar when we first discuss them, rather than shocking and anachronistic. Philosophy is not enough however. Several key teachings of Christianity are only accessible through scripture. We must first discuss the reliability of scripture from a historical perspective (Chapter 4). After this, we can get to the heart of the book and learn about Christianity directly (Chapter 5). Finally, I will look back and discuss where we have been, and look forward to discuss where we must go (Chapter 6).

CHAPTER 2:
Arguments Against Christianity

Before getting to the core arguments for Christianity, it is necessary to discuss the most common arguments against Christianity. This will not prove Christianity. It will only show that it has not been disproved. We must clear out false notions before we can build true ones. Note that these sections assume a fair amount of knowledge about what Christianity teaches. If you do not have this knowledge or do not have these objections to Christianity, skip to the next chapter and come back later.

2.1 Suffering

If God is loving and all powerful, why does he let us suffer so damn much? This is one of the most common and accepted arguments against Christianity. Suffering is one of the states that every human knows, regardless of religion, gender, age, or nationality. Every religion must incorporate an answer to this problem, and at first glance this problem causes the end of Christianity, because central to Christianity is a God of limitless love.

There are two possible solutions to this problem. The first is emotional, and the second is logical. Because the problem of pain is an emotional one, I will discuss the emotional argument first. Let us assume that we have no understanding of why suffering exists. Christian doctrine teaches, however, that God has shown us his total empathy. He became man in the form of Jesus Christ. He was not a God wearing a man suit, he was an actual man who could and did feel actual pain. While he was a man, he suffered and died in the most painful and humiliating way possible. Crucifixion is among the nastiest torture and execution methods that humanity has ever come up with. Not only that, it was us, his children, who did it to him. We do not necessarily understand why God will not take the pain from us, but Christians understand that he has taken the pain upon himself in its entirety.

The second solution to the problem of pain requires that we step outside of the circumstances of this world. Imagine that there was no pain in the world and that there had never been any. What reason would there have been for us to leave the jungle? There would have been none. Without the pain and struggle of life, there is no cause for us to improve ourselves. All of our advancement as a race comes from our attempts to overcome pain. Why would we invent farming if we always had enough to eat? Why would we love our neighbor if everyone would be happy (including him) if we hated him? Why would we search for God if no answers were necessary to make us feel fulfilled? Not only does pain lead directly to the maturity of the human race, it also leads to the maturity of very many individuals. In fact, it would be hard to imagine someone maturing spiritually, mentally, or physically without ever having felt pain.

God loves us so much, that he lets us hurt so that we may *grow* into God's form. This sort of transformation cannot occur without stimuli or if it is forced. We cannot be forced to be like God, because being free is a fundamental part of what God is. There is a good analogy for this. A good mother lets her children move out when they are old enough. She does this not because they will be safer. Many children make painful mistakes when they first leave home. She does this because she knows

9

that if she does not let them grow up, they will be a shadow of what they should be. They must know freedom and difficulty in order to truly become mature.

Objection 1:

Most "problem of pain" arguments use free will, but I do not. Why is that?

Reply:

My arguments actually do depend upon free will, even though it may not be that apparent at first glance. Without adversity *and* free will it is not possible to grow. Adversity is necessary to give a reason to grow, while free will is necessary for the growth to mean something. I give higher priority to growth and other arguments give higher priority to free will, but you cannot really have one without the other.

Objection 2:

My argument seems to work and all, but I seem to have forgotten about the innocents. How is this whole pain thing beneficial when a child, or other innocent, is the one doing the suffering and dying?

Reply:

First, how does a child's suffering help humanity to mature? All forms of suffering have causes, and in overcoming these causes, we as a race become more mature. In the case of cancer, we become disciplined and knowledgeable in pursuit of a cure. In the case of evil actions, we must become strong to contain and destroy the evil.

Second, how does a child's suffering help individuals? Those around the child are called to love the child by the trauma of the event. Few people are not moved by the suffering of a child, but many people are not moved by the happiness of a child. Also, many who are close to the child must find their inner strength in order to be able to handle the situation.

Third, how does a child's suffering help the child, especially if the child dies? I cannot explicitly answer this question. A common Christian belief is that there is a special place in heaven for the innocents – those who were unable to mature due to the circumstances of their lives. The concern I have with this is that it works as a "get into heaven free card." Usually entrance into heaven is the result of both God's saving grace and a person freely accepting God. A young child cannot freely accept God. However, realize that to God, the time before death and the time after death are much more connected than it is for us. There is no reason why God cannot correct the problems of this life in the next. Perhaps the child has an opportunity after death, but before heaven, where they can complete their maturity, albeit in a different manner. God takes care of the innocents in his own special way, whatever that may be. Because of God's loving nature, we know that they are not disposed of or forgotten about. He has not revealed the details to us.

Objection 3:
You can handle everyday suffering, such as bad jobs, bad relationships, and broken arms, but is this extreme pain stuff really necessary? Isn't moderate pain good enough to do the trick?

Reply:
In general, the greater the pain, the greater the potential is for growth. Consider U.S. soldiers during WWII. In many cases soldiers are not the nicest of men, but being at war can lead them to a deeper understanding of service. They were there to serve their country by defending their homeland from attack,

serve their allies by protecting and liberating their peoples, and serve their enemies by removing oppressive governments, planting democracy, and liberating their peoples. If they died, they died in an act of service, which is sanctifying in its own right. Now we can discuss the soldiers' families. If they gave, with love, their brothers, husbands, and sons for the benefit of foreigners, then they are already far on their way to sainthood. It is difficult to be a saint if the worst that you ever suffer is a cold or a bad day at work.

Objection 4:

Well, you don't have extreme suffering. Does that mean that you are not called to sainthood?

Reply:

No. You are still called to sainthood. You just don't have the "easy" path of suffering available to you. Suffering is merely a tool to increase love. You can still love, without having suffered that much first.

2.2 Bad Christians[1]

Another common argument against Christianity is the following: You know this man, and he is a Christian. He is also a liar and a cheat. Should you become a Christian and become like him? He isn't the only bad Christian you've known. And then there are all the Christians in the news who have to be thrown in jail because of their crimes. You shouldn't emulate them, should you? Finally, religious wars have caused all sorts of pain. Wouldn't we be able to get along better if there was no religion?

---

1   The arguments in this section borrow heavily from C.S. Lewis, *Mere Christianity*, Chapter 10.

As it turns out, these questions appeal to our emotions; and they are based in a logical fallacy. They assume that if one Christian is a bad person, then all Christians are bad people and that Christian teaching is flawed. This is the same fallacy as saying that because one Visigoth is a murderer, then all Visigoths are murderers and that Visigoth teaching is flawed. These statements clearly have no basis in logic. The question should be the following: When a person becomes a Christian, does the person become more moral? Also, when a person ceases to be a Christian, does he or she become less moral? More importantly, how will *you* change when you become a Christian? If you strive to emulate Jesus, you will become a more moral person. There is no way to emulate Jesus and become a worse person, because he is the best person that has ever walked on this Earth. Those Christians who do not improve are not attempting to emulate Jesus with any degree of seriousness. This means that they are missing one of the central tenets of Christianity and should not be taken seriously as Christians.

There is something else that I must say. When you compare the good atheist to the bad Christian, you make an implicit assumption. You assume that the good atheist is perfectly all right and does not need to be improved. This is only correct if Christianity is wrong. If Christianity is true, then the good atheist does have a critical flaw. He or she has rejected God. This is ironic, considering that God gave the atheist a good temperament, like he gives some strength and some good looks. In all actuality, having a naturally good temperament makes it harder to realize the need for God. The sinner will see the destructive power of sin in his or her life and will realize much sooner that he or she cannot make it without help. The sinner will then reach out to God. An atheist with a naturally good temperament will have a much harder time realizing his or her need because the atheist's sins are much more insidious. This atheist will rely on his or her good temperament instead of on God. The situation is similar with those who have other kinds of advantages, be it money, strength, intellect, or beauty. This point depends upon whether or not Christianity is true or false, which will be discussed later. I include it to motivate atheists and other non-Christians to learn more about Christianity and to realize that the truth or falsehood of Christianity is a critically important question.

2.3 Other Religions

2.3.1 Religions Are Not All Equal

In the United States, one of the most common arguments against Christianity is the following: All people, all races, and all religions are equal. Why should you believe Christianity's claims that it is the one true religion? This argument is powerful and common because of the culture in the United States. We enshrine equality above almost any other good. With some probing questions, however, we realize that all people cannot be equal. A murderer is not equal to a soup kitchen volunteer. What the founders of the United States actually intended is that everyone is equal under the law. They did not intend that everyone be treated equally regardless of what they did. Both a murderer and a volunteer live under the same law, but while the murderer is thrown in prison the volunteer is honored. This is how it should be. It is similar when we discuss political systems. Practically and ethically, the U.S. political system is superior to that of Nazism. If this is not obvious to you, I suggest that you imagine being born Jewish in a world ruled by Nazism. In addition, it is clear that different religions have different amounts of truth in them. A cult that demands that its members commit suicide is flawed in a way not replicated in any of the major religions. It is also reasonable to expect that one of the major religions has a better grasp of truth than the others, though the differences are not always as dramatic and will take more work to discover.

Now that we can admit the possibility that one religion is more correct than the others, we are in a better position to question whether or not Christianity is true. We must do this by analyzing the truth claims of Christianity to decide which claims are true and which are false. Of course, it is quite possible that no religion gets it perfect, but it is extremely unlikely that all religions have the exact same amount of truth in them. In this book, I am primarily concerned with proving Christianity to be true, and I do not analyze other religions in depth.

I must mention that it is certain that all religions cannot be 100% true. Religions contradict each other all the time. For example, Christians believe that Jesus is God become man; and Muslims believe that he is not God. These cannot both be true. Once I have proved something about Christianity, I have proved all contradictory views from other religions false. Alternatively, I will often prove a concept that is also in a different religion. In this case, I will have proved part of a different religion to be true.

2.3.2 Who Then Is Saved?

Christians believe that Christianity is the one true religion. Many non-Christians believe that most Christians believe that only Christians go to heaven. Some (misinformed) Christians also believe that only Christians are saved. Who do well-informed Christians believe to be saved? That is, who really makes it to heaven? Many non-Christians and nearly all Christians know the passage:

> Jesus said to him, "I am the way and the truth and the life. No one comes to the Father except through me." (Jn 14:6)

This states explicitly you are saved by God the Father through Jesus. Many think that this also says that you must have knowingly become a Christian in order to be saved. That is not what Jesus believes, so it is not what this passage means.

To know this more clearly, we must look at some of the other words of Jesus, which are quoted much less often.

> "If I had not come and spoken to them, they would have no sin; but as it is they have no excuse for their sin. Whoever hates me also hates my Father. If I had not done works among them that no one else ever did, they would not have sin; but as it is, they have seen and hated both me and my Father." (Jn 15:22-24)

If you have never heard of Jesus, you are not, by default, condemned. It is possible to be saved even if you have no conscious knowledge of Jesus. What if you live in rural China and your only experience of Jesus is that one missionary handed you a pamphlet? You may have rejected Jesus externally by throwing the pamphlet away, but accepted Jesus's message of love and service to God and others without realizing it, and hence be saved. God understands that some have little knowledge of him, through no fault of their own. He will not hold your non-Christian birth against you. However, you will still have your chance to choose to follow God. Just because you cannot point to the specific event or thought where God reached out to you does not mean that it never occurred. Those who respond and give themselves to God are saved. Those who reject God condemn themselves by their rejection. Now, in most cases, it is impossible for us to determine who is in which column, and it is not particularly healthy for us to be overly concerned with it. We should pull people towards Jesus when given the opportunity, but it is not usually proper or possible to state who is condemned and who is saved.

If it is possible for a non-Christian to be saved, why should you be Christian? First, you should be Christian because Christianity is true, as I will demonstrate later. Second, if you strive to be like Jesus, you will find joy. Third, you should be Christian because if you have been genuinely offered the truth and you rejected it, you may well be condemned. We are not all Chinese farmers. To those whom much is given, much is expected.

2.4 Miracles

One of the standard arguments against Christianity is that miracles do not exist; and because the Bible claims that they do, the Bible must be wrong. I must make two points. First, stating that miracles can never occur is not a scientific statement, so don't claim that it is. Science tells about what can be observed and repeated in a controlled experiment. If something cannot be observed in a controlled experiment, it is not science, but that does not mean that it is impossible. It is only not easily reproducible. My second point is that if only one man was raised from the dead in all of history, it would not be that surprising if you were not there to see it. So when most people differentiate between the normal and the miraculous, they are really just differentiating between the common and reproducible and the rare and not reproducible. Should we really ignore the data, just because it is rare? Now, don't misunderstand me, I agree that we must analyze these exceptions to the everyday very carefully.

David Hume, a famous atheist philosopher, ably attacked miracles in *An Enquiry Concerning Human Understanding* in 1748:

> When anyone tells me, that he saw a dead man restored to life, I immediately consider with myself, whether it be more probable, that this person should either deceive or be deceived, or that the fact, which he relates, should really have happened. I weigh the one miracle against the other; and according to the superiority, which I discover, I pronounce my decision, and always reject the greater miracle. If the falsehood of his testimony would be more miraculous, than the event which he relates; then, and not till then, can he pretend to command my belief or opinion.
>
> In the foregoing reasoning we have supposed, that the testimony, upon which a miracle is founded, may possibly amount to an entire

proof, and that the falsehood of that testimony would be a real prodigy: But it is easy to shew, that we have been a great deal too liberal in our concession, and that there never was a miraculous event established on so full an evidence.

The test that Hume gives is the correct one. That is, we should only believe in a miracle if the possibility of the witness is deceived or lying would be more "miraculous." We must apply this test to any proposed miracle. As it turns out, his final statement is incorrect, because there is at least one miracle where the miracle having occurred is massively more probable than the witnesses being deceived or liars. This case is the resurrection of Jesus (§ 5.1.2). Imagine that you have a group of friends that you know very well and trust. What would you think if they told you that they saw a dead man get up and order coffee? They were quite sure that he was dead first because of the gaping hole in his chest and the detail that he was not breathing. At first you would think that they were joking; but when you press them, you would realize that they really do mean it. That is to say, if a group of witnesses is completely trustworthy, anything, including a miracle, is more probable than them lying. If they are careful observers, you can also be assured that they were not deceived. This is the situation with the authors of the New Testament (§ 4.2).

Another miracle, of a different kind, deserves mention in this section.

1) A miracle is something that cannot be explained by the natural order.
2) The natural order does not explain itself.
3) Therefore, the natural order is a miracle.

That is, all existence is a miracle. You may be under the impression that physicists can explain the natural order. This is not the case. Physicists can explain what exists, and to some degree how something exists; but they cannot explain why something exists. If a set of laws is found to be consistent with the universe, then those laws are considered true. These laws can often, with more understanding, be described in terms of more fundamental laws, but the most fundamental laws can never be explained. This argument is related to the discussion of the boundaries of the universe (§ 3.3). You may have a more sophisticated definition of miracle: "Something that cannot be explained by the natural order, and could only have been caused by an intelligent being." The natural order also requires this intelligent being (God), but it takes more work to see this (§ 3.6).

Once we have accepted a miracle or two, other miracles suddenly become more possible. However, I still agree that we must hold proposed miracles to very high standards of truth before we believe in them. I do not need to discuss charlatans for you to understand the importance of not believing every miracle man that we come across. Each miracle must be carefully analyzed based on the evidence available.

CHAPTER 3:
Understanding Christianity, Using Philosophy

We now move on to a philosophical defense of Christianity, without reference to scripture. This has the value of allowing those who do not trust scripture to get a core understanding of Christianity anyway. At the same time, it helps prepare for the scriptural arguments to follow in chapter 5. Figure 1 is a map, detailing the philosophical foundation of Christianity. Each arrow indicates that a section depends upon a previous section. As you can see, the arguments are not entirely linear. In the text that follows, I go down the left branch before I go down the right branch. Use this map to keep the dependencies straight. In the left branch, we start with physics, learn that physics cannot explain the universe, and end with an understanding of God. In the right branch, we start with neuroscience, learn that neuroscience cannot explain consciousness, and then end with an understanding of the soul. In this way, we see that not only do science and religion not conflict, but a careful study of science leads to an understanding that our knowledge is fundamentally incomplete without religion. It is a fundamental property of science that it cannot explain God and the soul. It is not something that can be fixed with more scientific theories or experimentation. I will discuss this more as we go.

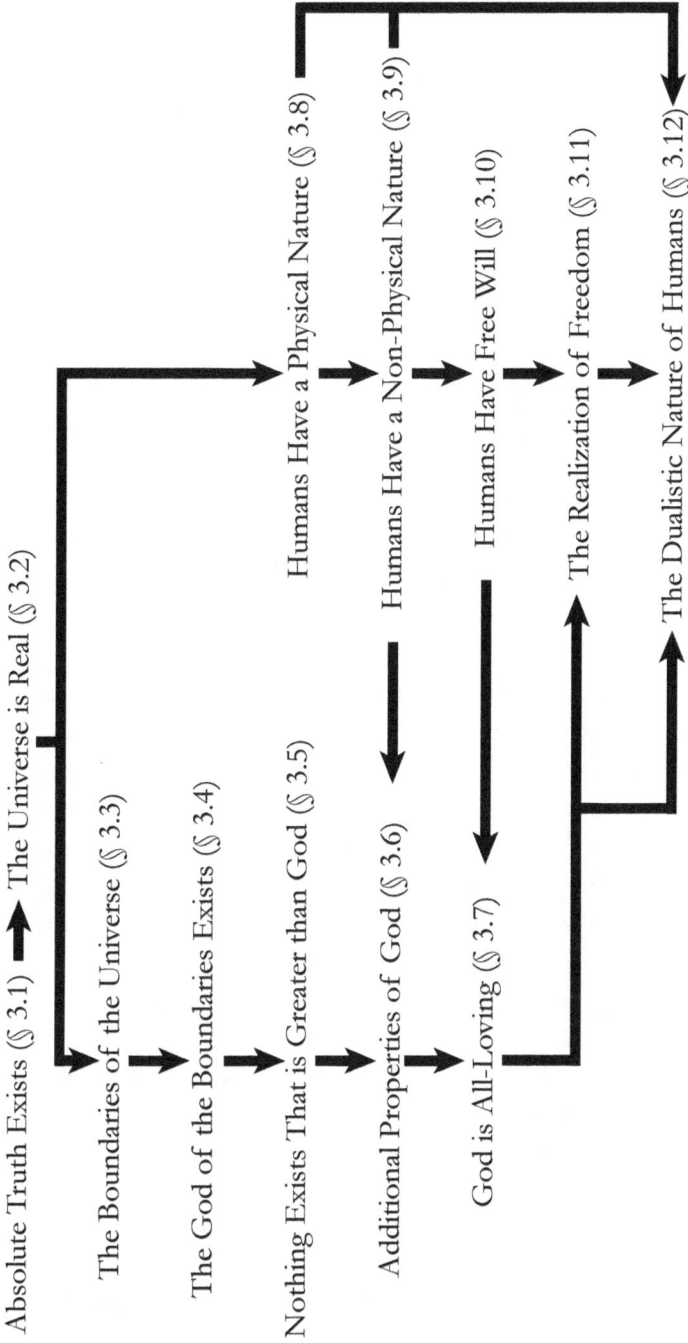

Figure 1 The Philosophical Defense of Christianity

Absolute Truth Exists (§ 3.1) → The Universe is Real (§ 3.2)

The Boundaries of the Universe (§ 3.3)

The God of the Boundaries Exists (§ 3.4)

Nothing Exists That is Greater than God (§ 3.5)

Additional Properties of God (§ 3.6)

God is All-Loving (§ 3.7)

Humans Have a Physical Nature (§ 3.8)

Humans Have a Non-Physical Nature (§ 3.9)

Humans Have Free Will (§ 3.10)

The Realization of Freedom (§ 3.11)

The Dualistic Nature of Humans (§ 3.12)

3.1 Absolute Truth Exists

I implicitly claim that every argument I make demonstrates the existence of an absolute truth. Absolute truth is something that is true independent of any observer. That is, it is true on its own, and does not depend upon the perspective or views of the person who claims the truth. In current thought, it is popular to say that absolute truth does not exist. When a culture says that something is true, it is not really true. It is only that which works for that given culture. For this reason, it is desirable to discuss the existence of absolute truth directly, rather than just by example. We can elegantly prove that absolute truth exists:

> **1)** Absolute truth does not exist.
> **2)** To be correct, the previous statement must be an absolute truth.
> **3)** Statements **1)** and **2)** contradict, so statement **1)** must be changed to "Absolute truth exists."

What this states, in so many words, is that "Absolute truth does not exist" is a self contradictory statement, and cannot be made true without changing the statement. I have not made any statement about how many absolute truths can be discovered. We must discover them one by one. If this argument makes you uncomfortable, look again at § 1.2.1 and realize that this argument follows directly from the self-consistency of truth.

3.2 The Universe Is Real

In eastern religions, the universe is usually presented as an illusion that we must escape from by being enlightened. Now, how do we decide if the universe is real or an illusion? Real objects are self-consistent. They don't disappear when you stop looking at them or look at them more closely. They are the same for every reasonable observer. They have properties that can be cataloged. Now let us see if these properties describe the universe. If they do not, the universe is an illusion, because an illusion does not require these properties, but reality does.

The universe is self-consistent. Whenever scientists find a contradictory statement in their theories, they are able to resolve the contradiction with time and effort. The problems are always found in the theories, not in nature itself.

When we close our eyes, the photons that compose light do not cease to exist. It is similar with all parts of nature that we have discovered. We do not need to observe a phenomenon or object for it to exist. When we look closer at the universe it reveals more detail, but it never starts to lose its reality.

Everything in the universe has properties that can be cataloged. Some of these properties don't change and some of them do; but they all have clear, identifiable properties.

All of these criteria describe the universe. Since the universe has all the properties of a real object and no identifiable properties of an illusion, we must say that the universe is real.

Now that we know that the universe is real, we can learn about the boundaries of the universe (§ 3.3) and the physical nature of humans (§ 3.8).

Objection 1:
We are brains in a vat, such as those in "The Matrix." What we think of as real has all of the properties I describe; but there is a deeper reality, which is the true reality.

Reply:
If there is a deeper reality, that does not conflict with the statement that our reality is also real. Once something has all the described properties of being real, we call it real. The definition given above is the most practical use of the term. If we required that something be the deepest reality before we call it real, then almost no philosophies or religions would call the universe real. Christians believe that God is the underlying reality, while most

atheists believe that our universe lies in some sort of higher structure of universes, and so forth.

3.3 The Boundaries of the Universe²

Now that we know that the universe is real, we can ask what the universe implies.

3.3.1 There Is At Least One First Cause

In nature, every effect has a cause that preceded it. A tree falls because it was chopped down. You are hungry because your body needs energy. The crops die because of the drought. With very little work, we see a problem. A tree falls down because it was chopped down. It was chopped down because a man was cold. A man was cold because it was winter. It was winter because of the position of the sun and the earth. The sun and the earth were where they were because they have been moving like a clock since they came into existence. They came into existence because of the laws of physics and the initial conditions of the universe. Hmm. What is the cause of the laws of physics and the initial conditions of the universe? Every causal chain eventually gets back to the question of what caused the universe. There may be more than one first cause (also referred to as an uncaused cause), but there must be at least one.

Objection 1:

The universe has existed for eternity. It has no first cause because it never began.

---

2 The arguments in this section borrow heavily from the five ways of St. Thomas Aquinas (*Summa Theologica*, I.2.3), who in turn borrowed from Plato (*Laws*, 893-6), and Aristotle (*Physics* VIII, 4-6 and *Metaphysics* (XII, 1-6).

Reply:

Current science has determined that this is not the case. First, there is very good evidence that the universe is around 13.7 billion years old and has evolved since its creation according to Big Bang Theory.[3] Second, there is a law of physics called the second law of thermodynamics, or the law of entropy. What it says is that the amount of disorder in the universe is always increasing and can never decrease. If the universe is infinitely old and disorder always increases, then the present universe would have zero order and be unable to support life. If the law of entropy breaks, many other laws, such as conservation of energy and the direction of time also break. Therefore, the entropy "clock" must have started at some point in the distant past, when the laws of physics were created. This is the beginning of the universe.

Objection 2:

There is an endless cycle of universe creation. Our universe was caused by another universe.

Reply:

This is possible. However, it does not avoid the problem. How did the first universe begin? Alternatively, perhaps there is an eternal series of universes. Then this eternal series of universes is the uncaused cause that caused our universe. There is no way of getting around the problem.

3.3.2 There Is At Least One Change Inducer

Everything in the universe is in motion. In order for anything to change, something else must change as well. For a car to

---

3   See, for example, www.talkorigins.org/faqs/astronomy/bigbang.html for an up-to-date, non-technical and correct explanation of big bang theory by Björn Feuerbacher and Ryan Scranton.

move, a person must fuel it and drive it. For a tree to grow there must be energy from the sun and rain falling from the clouds on a regular basis. For a star to be born, gravity must actively pull large quantities of space dust together. Again, if we push this train of thought, we quickly get to the boundaries of our understanding. Every change requires another change. A tree grows because sunlight falls on it. Sunlight falls on it because of the continuous nuclear reactions in the sun. There are nuclear reactions in the sun because atoms are being slammed together under the laws of physics. What gives the laws of physics the power to change nature? Every change depends upon another. Every change eventually depends upon a change inducer, or something that can change without being changed. There could be more than one change inducer, but there must be at least one.

3.3.3 There Is At Least One Existence Source

Everything in the universe depends on something else for its state of being. A person requires air to breathe. A plant requires sunlight to photosynthesize. A bed requires a floor to remain level and stationary. Nothing in our experience can depend upon itself for all that it needs to remain in its current state. Again, we run into a problem when we push this line of reasoning. You require air to breathe. The air requires gravity to be held near a planet. Gravity requires the reliability of the laws of physics. What do the laws of physics require? Soon, if we follow this type of chain, we must get to something that can sustain itself as well as sustaining something else. This is a source of existence. There may be more than one, but there is at least one.

3.4 The God of the Boundaries Exists

We know that the universe has boundaries. The First Cause of the universe must be a change inducer. If not, how could a change inducer be caused? How can this First Cause cause the universe without changing anything? This First Cause/Change Inducer must also be an existence source. If not, what caused the Existence Source? How does the First Cause exist without an existence source? I will call this First Cause/Change Inducer/ Existence Source the God of the Boundaries. To emphasize that we are not yet talking about a typical understanding of God, while reducing awkward language, I will shorten God of the Boundaries to GoB for the next several sections.

Be careful to realize how little I have actually shown. At this point, most faith traditions are consistent (but more detailed) with this conception of God. By faith tradition, I am including everything from pantheism (God is the universe), to panentheism (God has a soul, and a body, which is the universe, and they are interdependent), to deism (God is intelligent and created the universe but does not interact with the universe in any way except to keep the laws of physics running), to theism (God is intelligent and takes an active loving role in creation). To some degree, we have disproved atheism, but only if the atheist in question is very strict (denies the possibility of a first cause, change inducer, or existence source, even if that object is the universe).

Is it possible that there is more than one GoB which caused the universe? If this is the case, then these multiple GoBs must work together in perfect harmony to cause, induce, and sustain the universe. If they were not in harmony, they would be at war and the true GoB would win. What then caused the GoBs to work together? We must have another First Cause, who caused the necessary harmony. Of course, this means that the later GoBs are not GoBs at all, because they are no longer first causes. That is, there can only be one true GoB. A GoB composed of separate parts is self-contradictory. For the same reason, we cannot have a second GoB appear after the universe began.

Finally, we must realize that even though GoB is the root cause of all in the universe, it is not necessarily true that GoB controls everything in the universe. That is, even though no other can take control from GoB, there is no reason why GoB cannot give some control to others (such as humans). An analogy can help here. You have the power to place a pen on a specific location on your desk. If you drop the pen on your desk, you still caused the pen to arrive on your desk, but you did not control its final resting place. The laws of physics controlled that. Similarly, a father can make his son go to bed, but he can't make him sleep. If his son so chooses, he can stay up all night. If we have free will GoB causes many things about our lives, but we control the rest.

3.5 Nothing Exists That Is Greater Than God

No effect is greater than its cause. Here I use "greater" in the sense of "more remarkable in magnitude, degree, or effectiveness." To see that no effect is greater than its cause, consider some examples. If you put blue dye in water, the water will not get more blue than the dye. If you put water in the freezer, the water will not get colder than the air in the freezer. Parents must have life in order to give life to children. An entirely physical process cannot give a person a soul. That is, an object cannot give what it does not have (in either magnitude or nature).

Everything in the universe (or universes) has GoB as its original cause, existence source, and change inducer. Because no effect can be greater than its cause, the universe cannot be greater than GoB, nor can anything that is within the universe be greater than GoB.

That no effect is greater than its cause is a statement of great power, as the next section demonstrates. I will discuss first some common objections.

Objection 1:
GoB is greater than GoB's cause, so the effect can be greater than the cause.

Reply:
The rule describes a relationship between cause and effect. GoB is not an effect and has no cause, so the rule does not apply.

Objection 2:
Imagine an avalanche. Dropping of a tiny pebble can cause boulders to go careening down a hillside. Therefore, an effect can be greater than the cause.

Reply:
You assume that the dropping of the tiny pebble is the only cause. It is not. The other cause is the position of the rocks on the hillside: their large number, their distribution of weights, and their precarious position. Without all of these causes the avalanche would not have occurred. In many ways this is a physics problem, so we can discuss it with physics language. Before the avalanche, the rocks had potential energy, by reason of their position on the hillside. During the avalanche, the rocks have kinetic energy, by reason of their motion. After the avalanche, the energy has become heat energy and dissipated into the air and earth. At no point was any energy created or destroyed. That the effect was not greater than the cause is a way of saying that no energy was created, just changed.

Objection 3:

Imagine an atom bomb. A relatively small device has the power to flatten a city. Surely, the effect is greater than the cause.

Reply:

As it turns out, this is really the same objection as objection 1. What an atom bomb does is convert energy from mass into kinetic, light, and heat energy, using Einstein's relation $E = mc^2$, where E is the energy that gets released, m is the mass that gets transformed, and c is the speed of light. No energy gets created or destroyed, only changed.

Objection 4:

Humans evolved from single-celled organisms. Humans are greater than single-celled organisms, so the effect is greater than the cause.

Reply:

There are two possibilities here. First, let us assume that materialism is true. That is, that humans are merely the product of the laws of physics and the initial conditions of the universe. In this case, the objection is identical to objections 1 and 2. No energy was created or destroyed in the process of making a human; so in this way, a human is not greater than an equivalent quantity of single-celled organisms. You may say that what matters is not the energy, but the ordered complexity. Therefore, we must also discuss entropy. In any process in physics, it has been found to be true that the universe is never more ordered after a process than before. If you attempt to fight this process, you will create more disorder elsewhere. The classical simple example is to imagine two gasses, nitrogen and oxygen, divided by a partition. If you remove the partition, no energy has been lost; but the nitrogen and oxygen are thoroughly mixed, and therefore more disordered. If you replace the partition, the gasses do not sort themselves. Any process to sort the gasses is difficult, and will produce more disorder than it corrects. Similarly, as humans evolved more and more ordered complexity, other parts of the universe became less ordered. That is, if materialism is true, humans merely change energy from one form to another and reduce order. Note that the avalanche and the atom bomb also increase entropy, even though I did not discuss it as explicitly.

The other possibility is that humans have some non-physical component, that is, a soul. This soul cannot arise from evolution, because from physical causes only physical effects can come. The soul has a spiritual cause, which is GoB. The soul is the added value that allows humans to add value to the universe rather than remove it. I argue later (§ 3.12) that humans do indeed have a soul, but for now it is not assumed.

Objection 5:
There are strawberries in the universe. Therefore GoB is an ideal, very tasty strawberry.

Reply:
We have not shown that GoB is a strawberry. We have shown that GoB is greater than a strawberry. A strawberry gives nutrition, but GoB is the source of all life. A strawberry can give pleasurable sensations when it is eaten, but GoB is the source of that pleasure. GoB is not a strawberry, but GoB is the source of the essence of what makes a strawberry a strawberry.

Objection 6:
There is bat guano in the universe. This means that GoB is in some ways like the most perfect pile of dung that you have ever seen (very large, very stinky, and all disgusting).

Reply:
In some ways bat guano is like a strawberry. The bats used it to remove unnecessary material from their bodies; and it can

be used to nourish crops, so it is a source of life. The reply to the previous objection applies. It other ways bat guano is not a good thing. Be exposed to too much of it, and you will get sick. For that matter, if you eat too many strawberries, you will get sick as well. Both strawberries and bat guano have good and bad aspects. This is leading us directly to the next objection.

Objection 7:

There is good and evil in the universe. This means that GoB contains a perfect evil aspect as well as a perfect good aspect.

Reply:

This is a form of dualism. To a large degree, it is too early to discuss this, because I have not yet explained where good and evil come from (§ 3.10). However, this is where the current chain of objections leads. What we must realize is that existence is good, while non-existence is evil. Therefore, a "perfect" evil cannot exist. What then do we mean when we say "evil"? The key insight required here is that evil is the corruption of good. Evil is defined by what it is not (good) rather than by what it is. Asking where evil comes from is like asking where dark comes from. There is no source of dark. There are only sources of light, which do not necessary reach into every corner and room.

3.6 Additional Properties of God

We are conscious. Nothing exists that is greater than God. Therefore, God is conscious. All the power in the universe is pretty much wasted if you are not aware of it. There is no equivalency such that our consciousness is worth as much as the ability to create suns or some other grand power. This means that for God to be greater than us, God must be conscious. Sections after this one will use different language in a reflection of our new understanding of God. God can no longer be considered as an inanimate object, but must be seen as a being with self-knowledge and will. God's consciousness cannot be based in the physical universe, for the same reason that our consciousness cannot be based in the physical universe (§ 3.9).

It now becomes more accurate to refer to God as creator rather than merely cause. God, being the conscious will behind the universe, is the creator of the universe. There are two possibilities: 1) God created matter from God's will, and then used that matter to create the universe. 2) Matter is uncaused, and God formed that matter into the universe. In possibility two, matter is part of God, because everything that is uncaused is God (§ 3.4). However, we realize that the difference is largely one of semantics. In both cases, in the beginning there was only God (everything that is uncaused); and later there was God and the universe, shaped according to God's will. In both cases, the conscious, spiritual God is the one in control. In both cases, the universe is of God, but not fully God. Realize that we have defined the beginning to be the time when there were only causes and no effects. Whether or not matter existed in the beginning is now understood to not be an important question.

At this point, pantheism must be eliminated as a possible faith tradition because it claims that the universe is fully God. In addition, most forms of pantheism deny that God (the universe) is conscious. Panentheism must also be eliminated, because it treats God's soul and God's body as balanced and interdependent. This is not the case because God's spiritual nature is always in control. If God affects the universe, and then the universe affects God, it was what God intended all along.

We are now in a good position to describe many more properties of God.

God is immense. God is present everywhere in the universe(s), because God moves it (them) and sustains it (them). It is impossible to avoid God by traveling in space.

God is eternal. God is present at all times in the universe(s), for the same reason. It is impossible to avoid God by traveling in time.

Note, additionally, that modern physics (general relativity and especially Big Bang cosmology) teaches that matter, energy, space, and time are all tied together. When we talk about the universe before matter and energy, we must also conceive of a universe before space and time, and a time when the laws of physics that we are familiar with do not apply. This causes terms like "before" the universe and "outside" the universe to become awkward half-truths. It is more accurate to say that God is not bound by space or time. God can exist inside space and time because God created them, and has power over them, but that is not God's natural state. Not only does this mean that God exists everywhere in space simultaneously, but God also exists everywhere in time simultaneously. As a consequence, God knows the future as well as God knows the past, and God does not evolve or grow with time.

God is omnipotent. By omnipotent, I mean that there are no forces in the universe(s) that are great enough to move God. God created the universe(s) and God has total power over it (them), as God so desires.

God is omniscient. By omniscient, I mean that God is more knowledgeable than any and all other beings in the universe(s). If God is the cause of all knowledge, then nothing that is caused could learn more than God. However much we learn, we cannot learn as much as God.

Objection 1:

By making God conscious, I am making God in my own image. Isn't that awfully vain?

Reply:

I am not making God in my image. What I am saying is that God must be greater than I. This is a statement of humility, not vanity. It would be of greater arrogance to say that God is not conscious, because then I would have something that God does not.

Objection 2:

I define eternal, infinite, omnipotent, etc. a bit oddly. Normally people say all-powerful, all-knowing etc., without qualification, while I define these terms with respect to the universe(s). Why is that?

Reply:

As I have defined the terms, they are completely defendable. It is difficult to define (and therefore defend) God's properties "outside" of a universe, because I know very little about the "outside" of a universe. On one hand, Big Bang cosmology teaches us that asking about what God is like "outside" of a universe requires us to ask what God is like in a place with no space or time. On the other hand, we know that God existed "before" space and time, and as such God is not bound by them, and must exist "outside" them.

Objection 3:

God knowing the future contradicts free will.

Reply:

Just because God knows what will happen does not mean that he controls it. That is, just because I know that John Wilkes Booth killed Abraham Lincoln does not make me responsible for it. Just because I know that the sun will rise tomorrow does not mean that I cause it to happen.

Objection 4:

There are examples of God changing his mind (Amos 7:3, Jeremiah 18:8, Exodus 32:14). Since God changes with time, he must not exist equally at all times.

Reply:

It is more accurate to say that it appears to the prophet in question that God is changing his mind, while in actuality

God is placing a test upon the prophet, the city in question, or humanity. God knew all along that we were going to pass the test.

This does not mean that God is static like a rock or a corpse. It is closer to say that God is static like the ocean. That is, the ocean is always the ocean, but it is always full of energy and dynamism.

3.7 God Is All-Loving

When I speak of love, I refer to unconditional giving of self to another. This love is not romantic in nature, nor is it aesthetic pleasure such as you feel when you eat a good meal or see a beautiful painting. I am also not referring to the natural bond between persons who share common desires, interests, or familial associations. In the Greek Bible, the unconditional giving of self to another is referred to as agape. Throughout this book, when I say love, I mean agape. Because love (agape) exists in the universe(s), God's love must be greater (§ 3.5).

We should ask the question, "What exactly does God love?" Let us imagine the time when only God existed. This means that the only thing for God to love would be God's own self, since otherwise God would love nothing, and would not love.

Now move forward to when God created the universe. God created the universe in an act of will and love. Because God created the universe, and God loves God, God must love the universe, and everything in it (including us).

God is perfect in the absolute sense of the term. It is not possible to make God better (who could do this?), nor is it possible to create a being that is better than God (again, who could do this?). In this sense (the ontological sense) God is good. To be ontologically good means to be "true to your nature," or to be the best that you can be. God is the best God that can be, so the term is appropriate.

God also has absolute moral goodness. To have moral goodness means to want what is best and to act for what is best. God must be more (§ 3.5) good than the moral good that exists in the universe(s) (§ 3.10).

At this point, deism must be eliminated as a possibility because it denies, implicitly or explicitly, an all-loving God. We have arrived at a theistic understanding of God. Of the major religions, Christianity, Judaism, and Islam are all consistent with everything we have said so far. To further delve into a Christian understanding of God, we will need to learn from scripture (Chapters 4 and 5). Before then, we will learn about what it means to be human, using philosophy.

Objection 1:

I am basing my knowledge of God's loves on our loves. Are not our loves just a product of evolution? Does not our concept of good and evil come from evolution as well?

Reply:

Perhaps evolution had a hand in determining what we see as good, and what we love. After all, ants typically exhibit quite "moral" behavior. However, this does not change that God is the first cause. If evolution is true, then God caused it, which causes us to understand good, evil, and love. God is the first cause, not evolution.

Objection 2:

For that matter, none of these things really exist. Given inputs (environment) our program (genetics) determines what we will do (outputs). We have no choices in the matter. Ascribing morality to a non-free agent is an exercise in futility.

Reply:

We have free will (§ 3.10).

Objection 3:

Love is a weakness. To give of yourself unconditionally means to get less than you give. If God loves, God is less than God's creation. Therefore, God does not love.

Reply:

God cannot run out of love. Just as we have already seen with God being the first cause, change inducer, and existence source (§ 3.4), God does not need to get something before giving it away. It is hard to imagine a greater strength. Similarly, a key attribute of a saint is the ability to love without compensation. A saint, however, cannot do this without the assistance of another. This other is God.

3.8 Humans Have a Physical Nature

We know that the universe is real (§ 3.2). When we look at the universe using physics, we discover that it is composed of matter and energy. This matter and energy changes distribution and form according to the laws of physics. When we look at ourselves, we find that we are composed of the same types of matter and energy. A large fraction of the sun is hydrogen. A large fraction of each human is hydrogen. Much of the crust of the earth is oxygen. A large fraction of each human is oxygen. The difference between us and the sun and the earth is largely the exact percentages of each element, but more importantly, how those elements are connected to each other. In humans, oxygen, carbon, and hydrogen form highly-ordered chains and structures, while highly-ordered structures are typically not apparent in objects that are not alive.

Not only are the contents of humans similar to that of the rest of the universe, but both we and the universe are bound by the same laws of physics. In our brains are about 100 billion neurons. Each of these neurons pushes signals down its axon (output fiber) by pushing ions across boundaries in a specific electrochemical process. This process is well understood in terms of the laws of physics. When we eat, we extract chemical energy from the food; so that we may use it to walk, talk, and think. Every process in the body that has been scientifically measured is similarly bound by, and takes advantage of, the laws of physics. These same laws of physics can be used to understand electrochemistry in a battery, the motion of the planets, and nuclear reactions in the sun.

Can everything about humans be explained by physics? No. The complexity of humans, especially their brains, lies well beyond the means of experimental and theoretical science. However, this may just be a limitation of our current science. Materialists believe that humans are (or more accurately, everything is) entirely physical; every future discovery in science will confirm this; and future science will be similar in methodology to current science.

Note that many contemporary philosophers prefer the term physicalist, rather than materialist, because it highlights the connection of this philosophy with physics. Historical philosophers as well as contemporary and historical theologians typically use the term materialism. Because this is more of a theology book than a philosophy book, I will use the term materialism.

3.9 Humans Have a Non-Physical Nature

We have shown that humans are physical. Are they merely physical? Are the materialists correct that everything is entirely physical, including humans? Is all knowledge therefore physical knowledge? Can everything about humans be known (in principle) in terms of matter, energy, and mathematical laws? The key insight into these questions is the knowledge argument, put into current form by Frank Jackson.[4] This argument is motivated by the realization that human consciousness is special. Intuitively, there is something decidedly non-physical about consciousness. However, attacking the problem of consciousness directly is one of the more challenging problems in philosophy. For this reason, the knowledge argument looks at a simpler problem, that of qualia (to be defined in a moment). Because qualia themselves are difficult, we start with an even simpler problem, which is a thought experiment in which all reasonable people agree on the data, if not necessarily the interpretation.

We shift our focus here from physics to neuroscience, but the change in focus is not as great as it first appears because neuroscience (and all other science) is understood (as a fundamental principle of science) to completely reduce to physics. Imagine Mary, who is born completely color blind. In all other ways her vision and experiences are the same as any other human. As she grows up, she becomes interested in color, and becomes the world's pre-eminent color scientist. She understands photons, rods, and cones. She understands how the brain measures the first axis of color information given the signal on the red versus the green cones and how the brain measures the second axis of color information given the signal on the blue versus the red and green cones. She learns everything that physics and neuroscience can teach about color vision. Given any visual stimulus, she can experimentally determine what neurons fire in a given brain and measure what physical color information that person or animal acquires.

After she has learned all the physical facts about color, medical science advances to the point that her visual defect is completely corrected, so that she can now see color. Now when

---

4   Jackson, F. 1982, "Epiphenominal Qualia", *Philosophical Quarterly* 32: 127-136. Note that Frank Jackson arrives at a different conclusion based on this argument than I do.

she sees watered grass, she says, "Ah ha! So that is what it is like to see green." When she sees a ripe tomato, she says, "Ah ha! So that is what it is like to see red." She knew all physical facts before. She has learned a new fact: what it is like to see color. Therefore, there are facts in the universe which are not physical. We call these facts phenomenal. Not coincidentally, these new facts are tied to consciousness. The conscious sensations of seeing colors, feeling pains, sensing warmth, etcetera are referred to as qualia (singular: quale). Note that neuroscience has no place for consciousness,[5] even though we all are aware of it. This is the most important clue that neuroscience cannot tell us everything there is to know about being human.

Let us look more deeply at the knowledge argument. What does it mean when we say that a fact is unknowable using physics? What we mean is that no matter how many textbooks Mary looks at and no matter how many conversations she has, she will not be able to learn what red looks like without experiencing it for herself. That is, what it is like to see red cannot be communicated with language.[6] Physics is a mathematical language that describes nature, so it follows that anything that cannot be communicated with language cannot be communicated with physics.

Let us make our description of physics as a language more precise. Extrapolating from information theory (originally developed for computer science, but now applied to many fields, including physics and neuroscience), any distribution of matter and energy can be represented as a series of bits (that is, zeros and ones), where the bits are information. In order to see how the bits change with time, it is necessary to have operations (add, shift, etcetera) which act on the bits. These operations are used to represent laws of physics. Essentially, a fact can be

---

5   Chalmers, D.J., "Consciousness and its Place in Nature", in: *Philosophy of the Mind: Classical and Contemporary Readings.*

6   Hellie, B. "Inexpressible truths and the allure of the knowledge argument", in: *There's Something About Mary*, pp 333-64.

represented in the language of physics if, and only if, it can be represented with bits and operations. An ideal physicist can translate any measured distribution of matter and energy into bits, run these bits through the operations that represent the laws of physics, and translate the resulting bits into predictions about the probabilities that future measurements will return specified results. It follows that any field that reduces to physics (neuroscience, computer science, etcetera) can also in principle be expressed in its entirety with bits and operations. Mary could never learn what it is like to see red by looking at bits and operations. She must experience redness for herself. The knowledge argument teaches us that the epistemic power of physics, and therefore neuroscience, is limited; and it can never explain every known fact as the materialists expect it to.

Let us push the knowledge argument a bit further. Can an entirely physical brain know phenomenal facts? No. A physical brain stores information in bits (spiking activity, individual neuronal characteristics, and neuronal connections) and processes the bits with operations (spiking neurons cause others to spike, which can cause those neurons to change their characteristics, connections, or cause them to spike). The physical world stores information in bits (distribution of matter and energy) and processes the bits with operations (the laws of physics). With the knowledge argument, we demonstrate that knowable phenomenal facts exist and that physics (or any collection of bits and operations) cannot contain them. Because the physical brain only has the functional capabilities granted it by physics, it cannot contain phenomenal facts either.

I have focused the discussion on sensory qualia in order to make the problem of consciousness concrete. However, it is apparent that all aspects of consciousness lead to similar questions. We can ask: What is it like to add 1+1? What is it like to use language? What is it like to pursue an ideal? What is it like to love? You can imagine building arguments similar to that of the knowledge argument for each domain, though as the topic becomes more abstract the thought-experiments become less intuitive. More simply, though, it is apparent from our experience that all aspects of consciousness have a shared nature, and therefore must have a similar non-physical origin.

It is also apparent that consciousness includes not only knowing "what it is like" but all non-physical knowledge. This includes knowing who you are or I am. It includes knowing what trees are, physics is, or how to do philosophy. It includes knowing God. A physical brain can only store and process physical information, while a non-physical mind is necessary for non-physical knowledge. The distinction between information and knowledge can be subtle in many specific cases, but there is no doubt that in general there is a distinction.

Next, we will discuss free will. Later (§ 3.12), we will discuss the balance between the physical and phenomenal nature of humans in more detail.

Also realize that this argument implies that any conscious being, including God, must have a non-physical nature (§ 3.6).

Objection 1:

St. Thomas Aquinas says (*Summa Theologica* I.75.3) that sensory experience is inherently physical because it requires a body, while the intellect is inherently non-physical and does not require a body.

Reply:

The front end of seeing is indeed physical. This is the process by which light is caught by photoreceptors and transmuted into electrical-chemical impulses in the retina and brain. However, the back end is non-physical. This is the part where we become conscious of what we are seeing and "know what it is like." Note that the act of seeing does not intrinsically require the awareness of seeing, as robots can process color, but have no awareness.

The front end of thinking is also physical. Aquinas refers to this as the cogitative power or particular reason, which includes comparison, computation, and memory. He correctly understands that its source is physical. "Wherefore it is also called the particular reason, to which medical men assign a certain particular organ, namely, the middle part of the head" (*Summa Theologica* I.78.4). The back end of thinking is non-physical. Aquinas refers to it as the intellect and it includes both consciousness and knowledge (*Summa Theologica* I.75.2). The cogitative power does not intrinsically require consciousness and knowledge, as a robot can compute, but cannot know. Present day philosophers typically refer to the intellect as the mind, and the cogitative power as the brain.

Objection 2:
What is the status of animals?

Reply:
Many measured systems in animal brains exhibit substantial unpredictability. Most of this unpredictability we can expect to eventually explain with purely physical reasoning. On the other hand, neuroscience does not assure us that there is no hidden variable, the non-physical mind, which is influencing the physical brain. Anything we can understand completely using physics we can state to be physical. Currently, isolated electrons, rocks, computers, planets, etcetera all qualify. Simpler organisms, such as plants (which have no brain) and sea slugs (which have about 20,000 neurons), we can also reasonably expect are completely physical based on current experimental knowledge. As experimental techniques improve, the number of systems that can be completely explained with science will increase. It is also possible, in principle, that we will eventually be able to measure explicitly that a human mind cannot be explained entirely in terms of physics. For now, though, we can understand ourselves to have a non-physical nature because

we have insider information (our own consciousness). We can safely assume, by analogy, that other humans are also conscious and have a phenomenal nature. For most animals, however, I lack the philosophical and scientific tools to make a clear determination.

3.10 Humans Have Free Will

The materialist view, taken to its natural conclusion, asserts that there is no free will. Neuroscience typically assumes this view, which it inherits from physics. It is reasonable to argue this way when discussing ants that cooperate for the greater good of the colony. It is reasonable to use it when discussing why a mouse chooses to go one way in a maze rather than another. It is necessary, but not quite as reasonable, to use it when discussing which medications we should give a person with severe depression. It is not necessary, even harmful, to use it when discussing what motivates a sane person to kill another or sacrifice his or her life for another. It becomes harmful because it turns us into animals with no reason and no responsibility. That is, it states that people are no more than complicated ants. I have shown that humans have both a physical and a non-physical side. Because we know that the laws of physics do not take into account humans' non-physical side (and are therefore fundamentally incomplete), there is no particular objection remaining to humans having free will. However, we must still ask, can we argue that humans do have free will?

Look again at the knowledge argument. How do I know what it is like to see red? That is, how can I have a conscious awareness of redness? I can actually see red. If I was color blind from birth, you could never explain to me what it is like to see red. Similarly, I know what it is like to choose freely. I am familiar with the sensation of free will. If I had never been free, I would not know what it is like; and you could not explain it to me. Essentially, having free will is a necessary requirement for knowing what it is like to be free. Because we know what it is like to be free, we are free.

Freedom implies choice. Choice implies that there is a better and worse choice, because if choices do not lead to better or worse outcomes, then freedom is purely illusory. We define better choices to be good and worse choices to be evil. This knowledge of the existence of good and evil (which is really the existence of freedom) informs our understanding of God (§ 3.7). After that, we can ask in the next section how we should use our free will.

3.11 The Realization of Freedom

We understand that humans have free will. How should we apply this freedom? At this point, it is helpful to differentiate three kinds of freedom. First, freedom of will is the ability to desire this or that action. It must, by its nature, exist outside the laws of physics, because the laws of physics do not contain any concept of will, only determinism and randomness. Because we have freedom of will, and freedom of will is not physical, it must be based somewhere other than our physical bodies. As a corollary, freedom of will cannot be lost by any physical mechanism, such as imprisonment. However, you can use your freedom of will to choose to ignore your freedom. By losing hope, you can allow your body and your environment to determine your actions and your fate. Freedom of will is also called metaphysical freedom and is the type of freedom that is most often discussed in philosophy.

Second, freedom of action is the ability to actually do this or that action. Freedom of action can be lost, for example, through addiction, imprisonment, or fear. As freedom of will is misused, freedom of action is lost. As you use drugs or pornography, your body builds up a chemical dependence. Even if you want to stop, the addiction builds a physical barrier that can be extremely difficult to overcome. As you steal or murder, you will be imprisoned. As you lie, you will not be trusted with responsibility. If you abuse your free will, you violate that which is called natural law. It was built into nature by God as the creator of nature. The vast majority of the universe has no choice but to obey God's will. When a rock is dropped, it falls. It does not have a choice in the matter. For a rock, the law of nature is absolute. However, we do have a choice, so for us the law of nature is not absolute. There is, though, a penalty for breaking God's law. Aside from the pain that usually results, there is a loss of freedom of action. Freedom of action is also called physical freedom, and is the type of freedom most often discussed in politics or economics.

Third, freedom of realization is the ability of an action to affect reality. Freedom of realization is lost when your actions are not consistent with the expectations of the environment. For example, if you are in a healthy company, designing a useful device will cause that device to be produced and sold by the company. When your device is sold to millions, your actions have been realized. If you are in an unhealthy company, designing a useful device may cause you to be fired, and your actions will never be realized. In a much more fundamental sense, freedom of realization is lost when your actions are not consistent with God's will. Which will cause you to have a greater influence in the world, to work with or against the master of creation? In the short term, it may seem to make sense to turn against God, but in the long term there is only God. It is great foolishness to cleave to that which is temporary and struggle against that which is eternal.

So we see that if we want to maximize freedom of action and freedom of realization, we must turn our freedom of will towards God. This statement is in conflict with popular opinion in the Western world, where freedom is defined as doing whatever you want, as long as it does not directly hurt other people. In practice, however, other people often excludes those such as the unborn, because of "the freedom to choose," or the poor, because of "the freedom of the market." A proper understanding of freedom leads us to realize that the greatest freedom comes from turning towards God. Any other action leads to less freedom.

The natural law is written by God in our bodies, our minds, and in the very structure of the universe. Does this mean that we can follow whatever urges we have, because they are "natural"? No. We must check our urges to see if they are in tune with the design of the universe. If they are, they should be encouraged; and if they are not, they should be resisted. To pick one example, even though a mother may desire to kill her child, it is not correct. Her body was designed to have children. Without children, the human race dies. When she breastfeeds, her body releases the hormone oxytocin, which leads to bonding. This tells us that it is natural for a mother to take care of her child and unnatural to do her child harm.

At times, the law of nature is not easy to interpret. However, there is another law, the greater one, which can be learned by looking at God's nature more directly. We know that God is all-knowing (§ 3.6), so God can tell good from evil, and all-good (§ 3.7), so that God loves good. Therefore, that which God loves is good. It is best if we love what God loves. This means that because God loves God's own self, it is good to love God; and because God loves God's creation, it is good to love God's creation; and because God loves us, it is good to love each other and ourselves. It is evil to do the reverse of these things.

Now, why does God allow us to go against God's will? Wouldn't we be good if we could not choose evil? God's love for us is great enough, that God will allow us to turn away from God, if we so desire. If, in the end, we return God's love, it will be greater because it was freely given. "No one can act rightly except by free choice of the will, and God gave us free choice in order to enable us to act rightly."[7]

---

7   St. Augustine, *On Free Choice of the Will*, § 2.18.

3.12 The Dualistic Nature of Humans

What form does the interaction between humans' physical (§ 3.8) and phenomenal (§ 3.9) natures take? We can get the known possibilities from David Chalmers's discussion of the topic.[8] We have already shown that the physical affects the phenomenal. Does the phenomenal affect the physical? Yes. This is how Mary can say, "Ah ha! So that is what it is like to see red." To contradict this, an epiphenomenalist (the position that I am arguing against) must resort to extreme measures. The epiphenomenalist must say that seeing the tomato caused Mary (§ 3.9), by a purely physical pathway, to say, "Ah ha! So that is what it is like to see red," and also, by a separate phenomenal pathway, caused Mary to have the sensation of seeing red. If this is the case, how does Mary know that she actually had the sensation of seeing red? She does not. Her physical mind has never had access to the phenomenal experience; and as such her physical mind has no way of verifying that the phenomenal experience actually occurred. Any physical reports (Mary verbally telling herself what she feels) are therefore unreliable. Therefore, an epiphenomenalist must hold that no facts about qualia are knowable. However, a premise of epiphenomenalism is that facts about qualia are knowable. Therefore, by the law of non-contradiction (§ 1.2.1), epiphenomenalism is false.

Is it possible that after physical minds evolve sufficient complexity, that phenomenal properties emerge spontaneously, and that these properties influence the physical mind, as described by property dualism? No. In physics, there is no such thing as spontaneous emergence. The properties of gases can be derived from the properties of atoms using statistical mechanics. The properties of stars can be derived from the

---

8   Chalmers, D.J., "Consciousness and its Place in Nature", in: *Philosophy of the Mind: Classical and Contemporary Readings*.

standard model plus general relativity. If something appears to arise spontaneously, then either it has some non-physical cause, or the physics of the situation is not understood. If property dualism were true, then phenomenal properties would be a direct consequence of physical properties; and once Mary knows all the physical facts about the mind; Mary could derive all of the phenomenal facts as well, and she would learn nothing upon being healed. If the phenomenal is a direct consequence of the physical, we should reclassify the phenomenal as physical, and property dualism becomes incoherent. Essentially, the "phenomenal" becomes just one more gear in the materialist machine.

At this point, we must accept that the physical and the phenomenal natures of the mind interact and that the phenomenal is not wholly dependent on the physical. For completeness we should also ask, is the physical aspect of the mind wholly dependent on the phenomenal? No. For this to be the case, my (or our) phenomenal mind (or minds) would have to determine the contents of my physical mind, including its genetics. This would require that my mind (or our minds) determines who my parents are, and their parents are, all the way back to the beginning. This requires at least two extremely non-intuitive things. The first is that I created (or assisted in the creation of) the universe, an event of which I have no memory or apparent ability. The second is that I (or we) created laws of physics that are intricate, extremely surprising to us, and self-consistent when applied in the appropriate regime.

Now we know that both the phenomenal and physical contribute to what it means to be human, and neither of these aspects is based entirely upon the other. Let us consider the case of neutral monism. Neutral monism asserts that all fundamental particles (electrons, photons, quarks, etcetera) have an intrinsic phenomenal as well as a physical nature, just as particles have both a wave and a particle nature. If a physicist asks if an electron is a particle or a wave, the correct answer is somewhere between both and neither. The question is badly defined. An electron has properties of both a wave and a particle, but it is only one object. That we call an electron a "particle" is a historical accident because that is how they were first observed. Physicists understand that this is not correct, and a different name such as wavicle would be better, but no such name has caught on. Similarly, a neutral monist asserts that when you ask if a particle is physical or phenomenal, the correct answer is somewhere between both and neither. There is only one object, with one nature, that has different properties depending upon how you look at it. That we call an electron "physical" is a historical accident, because that is how we usually observe them. It is not necessary for an electron to be conscious in the way that we are conscious. As particles come together to build up a body at some point the ordered complexity of the physical properties of the particles causes the phenomenal properties of the particles to synchronize and form what we think of as consciousness. Neutral monism is contrasted from property dualism in that the particles in neutral monism already have a phenomenal nature which is synchronized by the physical, whereas in property dualism the phenomenal nature arises from the physical only. In neutral monism, it is irrational to suppose that unified consciousness survives death, or that there is any such thing that could be called a soul. The phenomenal decomposes along with the physical as the particles of the body come apart. Later, the particles recombine in a new form when they are taken up by other organisms. However, neutral monism cannot be correct, because we know that God loves us (§ 3.7). A loving God would not give us life and make us conscious, only to destroy us.

Only one philosophy listed by David Chalmers remains. Substance dualism asserts that there are at least two basic substances in the universe, physical and phenomenal, and that they interact in the mind. Understanding how and when God connected the two substances to each other is not required to understand that this model is acceptable. For comparison, realize that physicists do not need to know how and when God assembled the laws of physics to observe that they exist. All of the objections brought forth for the other philosophies do not apply to substance dualism. The physical nature of humans is typically called the body, and the phenomenal part is typically called the soul. We need the soul to direct the body, and the body to interact with the universe. Philosophically, our afterlife takes place in a new universe. Our soul will survive death as required by God's love, and our bodies will be rebuilt so that we may live in the new universe. To believe otherwise would be to assert that an all-loving God would leave us as half-dead ghosts. Realize that this statement, that both a soul and a body are necessary to be fully alive, is an official Christian teaching. The teaching that the soul is the true self while the body is a disposable shell is Platonism, not Christianity. At this point, it is appropriate to stop saying phenomenal and start saying spiritual when we speak of the part of person that is not physical.

We have now reached the end of my discussion of the Christian faith, without reference to scripture. If you are familiar with Christian doctrine, you will note that much is still missing. For these other teachings, we must refer to scripture, which we turn to next.

CHAPTER 4:
The New Testament

4.1 Authorship and Dating[9]

Before we can talk about what the New Testament says, we have to justify that what it says can be trusted. We must understand as much as we can about the authors of the New Testament and when they wrote it. The authors must have clear links to the eyewitnesses (or be eyewitnesses) to reduce the possibility of communication mistakes. We will learn that even in the most pessimistic, but rational, reading of the data, we come to the understanding that the authors of the New Testament are close enough to the events to be able to give an accurate picture of historical events. Much will be uncertain; but this we will know; and this is what we need in order to continue our investigation of scripture and Christian history.

---

9   My sources for this section and its subsections are Donald Guthrie, *New Testament Introduction*, Raymond E. Brown, *An Introduction to the New Testament*, the 2003 version of the *New Catholic Encyclopedia*, the book *The New Testament Documents: Are They Reliable?* by F.F. Bruce, and the writings of the church fathers (http://www.newadvent.org/fathers). I also used bits and pieces of various web sources, such as that of Glenn Davis (http://www.ntcanon.org) and Mahlon H. Smith (http://virtualreligion. net/primer), to help fill out some of the details.

Much of the information we have about the authors of the
New Testament comes from the church fathers, the leaders
of the church in the post-apostolic age. There is an unbroken
chain of writers discussing the New Testament that goes back
to soon after the Gospels were written. The writings of the
church fathers are referred to as "the tradition" or as "patristic
sources" in most discussions of this subject. For my purposes
I will look at the most relevant information from before A.D.
430. All information from after this time either depends on
earlier available sources or is suspect because we are unable to
determine what the earlier sources are.

Unfortunately, the questions of New Testament authorship
and dating are not cut and dried. The church fathers did not
have the current understanding of history and authorship. They
did not use footnotes or copyright dates. They rarely list their
sources. There is substantial variation in the writings of the
church fathers. To determine New Testament authorship as best
we can, we use the earliest of the patristic sources augmented
by the internal evidence of the New Testament.

In order to be able to use the patristic traditions to glean
information, we must have a clear understanding of how their
traditions changed with time. At the origin of a tradition, there
is the true story. This is what actually happened. Those who
see or experience the events (eyewitnesses) tell others (second-
hand witnesses) about it. The second-hand witnesses tell third-
hand witnesses and so forth. Each retelling can be either oral
or written.[10] With each retelling, there are a certain number of
mistakes made. That is, the true story gets corrupted. Because

---

10   In oral cultures, oral traditions are stable in a way that can be
surprising to those who have not experienced such traditions. However,
it is not as surprising when we realize that oral cultures contain the
entire wisdom and history of their people in oral form, so much care is
employed. See Bailey, K.E. "Informal Controlled Oral Tradition and the
Synoptic Gospels," *Themelios* 20.2 (1995) for a fascinating and informative
look into current middle-eastern oral culture.

each witness tells many of the next generation of witnesses, and each make different mistakes, there becomes many different, though related, traditions. The more important a tradition is, the more stable it is, because people are more careful when they give and receive it. The more people that know and agree on a tradition, the more stable it is, because they correct each other. Also, we must remember that not every tradition gets retold. If a tradition is not believed, or is considered unimportant, it will not be repeated. The traditions that get pruned will be those that are the least popular, but not necessarily the least true. In summary, over time traditions split and are pruned. The dominant tradition will then be subject to drift as traditions grow and split in one place and are pruned in another. Therefore, in order to keep the true story, it is critical that the tradition gets frozen before too much time has passed. When we have many traditions available, we can use this model to analyze the relevance of each tradition.

Note that it is popular among certain Bible scholars to discount the patristic tradition as a matter of course and rely only on the biblical texts themselves to determine questions of authorship and dating. This is silly for several reasons. The Bible was not handed to us by God in A.D. 1800. Much can be learned from what has been written about it in the preceding millennia. Today's man is not so much more knowledgeable and less biased than ancient man. Especially for the ancient tradition, we can expect that the church fathers actually had information that is not available to us by virtue of how close they were to the events themselves. Textual criticism of the New Testament can be problematic because it lends itself very strongly to non-conclusive arguments that depend more on the assumptions of the critic than the text. There are exceptions to this, but those exceptions are uncommon. In general, I will take the position that the patristic tradition is authoritative, unless the tradition itself is murky or it is contradicted by a clear and convincing textual argument from the New Testament.

4.1.1 The Tradition

Below are the most important church fathers with respect to the authorship and dating of the New Testament. For the most part, I will quote only these unless the record is thin or conflicting.

Papias (late 1st cent. - mid 2nd cent.) was a bishop of Hierapolis. He wrote a five book series, *Interpretations of the Sayings of the Lord*, which has now been lost except for quotations in later books, which are referred to as the fragments of Papias.

The Muratorian Fragment (ca A.D. 170) is not a church father, exactly, but a document. It is the oldest list of the books of the New Testament. The document itself is in bad shape, so for the most part it is difficult to interpret the absence of a particular book from this list. A book being on the list is a fair indication that it was in widespread use, however. It is dated because the author refers to the recent episcopate of Pius I of Rome, who died in A.D. 157.

Irenaeus (A.D. ca. 130 - ca. 202) was a bishop of Lyons. His preserved writings argue primarily against the Gnostics, a heretical splinter group. Because of the theme of this writing, he spent more time discussing sources than most writers of this era.

Clement of Alexandria (A.D. ca. 150 - ca. 213) was the head of the catechetical school in Alexandria. He should not be confused with Clement of Rome, one of the first popes.

Tertullian (A.D. ca. 160 - ca. 225) was primarily a writer of which many works are preserved. He converted to Christianity in middle life, but split away from the main church late in life largely because the church was not strict enough to suit him.

Origen (A.D. ca. 185 - ca. 253) was the head of the catechetical school in Alexandria after Clement. He left there as a result of a conflict (more political than theological) with the local bishop, and founded a new school in Caesarea.

Eusebius (A.D. 263-339) was bishop of Caesarea and the first true church historian. He preserved much of the tradition that would have been lost otherwise.

Jerome (ca. A.D. 347-419 or 420) was a priest and ascetic who moved frequently and wrote on many topics relevant to the church. He was the primary creator of the Vulgate, a key Latin translation of the Bible from Greek and Hebrew sources.

Augustine (A.D. 354-430) was a convert to Christianity and became bishop of Hippo. He was one of the great theologians of the church, and he also reported on historical details. In this time (and largely under the influence of Jerome and Augustine) there were several councils that ratified the contents of the current Roman Catholic Bible. As such, this is a natural time to end the discussion of the tradition. Practically speaking, the vast majority of the canon was accepted as soon as it was written, but there were several books with more controversial histories that took longer to accept or reject.

4.1.2 The Synoptic Gospels

The Gospels of Matthew, Mark, and Luke show dramatic similarities. When displayed in three columns, with Matthew on the left, Mark in the middle, and Luke on the right (*Gospel Parallels* Throckmorton), it becomes apparent that there is a significant relationship between the Gospels. They frequently describe the same events, have events in the same order, and use the same wording in a way that implies written dependence rather than oral dependence. Understanding the source of these similarities is referred to as the synoptic problem. The dominant understanding is that Matthew and Luke both separately had access to Mark, but not to each other. Mark's language is awkward or problematic in many cases. Both Matthew and Luke fix this language, but often in different ways. Similarly, Matthew and Luke often modify the order of events in Mark, but not in the same way. That is to say, for passages that are in all three Gospels, Matthew agrees with Mark and Luke agrees with Mark much more than Matthew agrees with Luke against Mark.

Both Matthew and Luke agree with each other, however, on content that is not in Mark. The understanding here is that there is another source, called Q by scholars, that both Matthew and Luke had. Q is primarily composed of sayings of Jesus. It is not expected that Matthew or Luke used each other because of the significant number of otherwise inexplicable omissions and conflicts between Matthew and Luke in how they use Mark and Q.

Finally, there is material that is unique to Matthew and other material that is unique to Luke. These are referred to as M and L, respectively. What we have described is called the four source hypothesis, where Mark, Q, M, and L are the sources. It is also often referred to as the two source hypothesis, where Mark and Q are the sources, and M and L are assumed.

Also apparent is that the author of John did not use the other Gospels as sources, and the other Gospels did not use John as a source. John almost never uses the same words to describe events and only occasionally describes the same events. It is likely that John was aware of the other Gospels, because his was the last written (see below). However, he was more concerned about recording what the others did not write about than what they did.

Now let us look in more detail at each of the books themselves.

The Gospel According to Mark

Summary of the Tradition

Papias: Mark was the interpreter (translator) of Peter, and he was very careful to record the true story (Eusebius's *Church History* 3.39.15).

Muratorian Fragment: The fragment indicates that there are four Gospels, but the surviving text only names the Gospels of Luke and John.

Irenaeus: Mark, the disciple and interpreter of Peter, wrote after the death of Peter and Paul (*Against Heresies* 3.1.1).

Clement: Mark wrote Peter's teachings while Peter was alive. Peter did not urge this on or forbid it. He wrote after Matthew and Luke, but before John (Eusebius's *Church History* 6.14.5-7).

Tertullian: Mark was the interpreter of Peter (*Against Marcion* 4.5).

Origen: The second Gospel was that according to Mark, who wrote it according to Peter's instructions. Peter also acknowledged Mark as his son in his general letter, saying in these words: "She who is in Babylon, chosen with you, sends you greetings; and so does my son Mark" (1 Pt 5:13; Eusebius's *Church History* 6.25.5).

Jerome: Mark was a disciple and interpreter of Peter. He wrote a Gospel that Peter approved of, as Clement and Papias said. Peter mentioned Mark (1 Pt 5:13). Mark died in the eighth year of Nero (61 AD) and was buried in Alexandria (*Illustrious Men* 8).

Augustine: Mark wrote second and summarized what Matthew wrote (*Consensus of the Gospels* 1.2.4).

Authorship

Here we can see the evolution of tradition that I described in my model (§ 4.1). Note that Irenaeus and Clement, who were contemporaries, agree about who wrote the Gospel, but not when. Because they do not agree completely, we know that they are not quoting the same source. They also have information that does not come from Papias, so their traditions are independent of Papias. However, they do agree on who wrote the text. This tradition is very wide, which is to say that all branches of the tradition point back to it, and very early. Because the traditions must intersect, they intersected before the time of Papias. Because the tradition that Mark, the interpreter of Peter, wrote the Gospel was started before Papias, it must have existed before the end of the first century. As I will defend momentarily, this is only a little later than when the Gospel was written. Therefore, we can be confident that it is true. By the time of Jerome and Augustine, the tradition had diverged still further. Because they are rather late in their testimony, I disregard what they say in favor of the earlier sources.

Dating

Now, when was this Gospel written? The confusion about whether it was written before or after the deaths of Peter and Paul implies that it was written around the time that they died in A.D. 67.[11] If he wrote both well before or after this time, there should not be any confusion in the tradition. Based on this, I date the Gospel as being written sometime between A.D. 55 and 75. The same constraint applies to Luke (discussed in the next section). That is, it was written before A.D. 75, and Mark

---

11   Finegan, *Handbook of Biblical Chronology*, § 672

was written before Luke (by the two source hypothesis), so we must change the dating of Mark to between A.D. 55 and 70.

Some Weak Alternative Theories

It used to be widely believed by the church that the author of Mark is the John Mark of Acts of the Apostles and the letters of Paul (Acts 12:12, 12:25, 13:5, 13:13, 15:36-40; Col 4:10; 2 Tm 4:11). There is no strong evidence for this. As you can see from the summary above, there is no early tradition saying that John Mark is the author of Mark. John Mark was an inhabitant of Jerusalem and an associate of Peter and Paul. John Mark's association with Peter was probably the source of this tradition, but there is no reason why Peter could not have two associates named Mark.

Many non-Christian scholars assert that it is impossible that Mark wrote before A.D. 70, because in the Gospel Jesus predicts the destruction of the temple that occurred in A.D. 70 (Mk. 13:1-2). I have two problems with this. The first is this assumes that prophecy, a fairly weak form of miracle, is not possible. This is assuming what we are trying to establish – whether God ever interacts directly in human affairs – to be no. This is a bad assumption (§ 2.4). The second problem I have with this belief is that it did not take a miracle to make this prediction. It could widely be seen that the Jews and the Romans were headed for a collision, and the Jews were not going to win any confrontation. The evidence of the tensions between the Jews and the Romans is substantial both in biblical and in non-biblical sources.

The Gospel According to Luke and The Acts of the Apostles

Summary of the Tradition

Papias: No comment from Papias has survived.

Muratorian Fragment: Luke, a physician, whom Paul had taken as one zealous for the law, wrote the third Gospel and Acts of the Apostles.

Irenaeus: Luke recorded the teachings of Paul after the deaths of Peter and Paul. He wrote after the Hebrew Matthew, at around the same time as Mark, and before John (*Against Heresies* 3.1.1). Irenaeus quotes Acts of the Apostles, with attribution to Luke as the traveling companion of Paul (*Against Heresies* 3.14.1).

Clement: Luke was written before Mark and John and at the same time as Matthew. When taken with Clement's writing on Mark, this means that Peter and Paul were alive at the time (Eusebius's *Church History* 6.14.5-7).

Tertullian: Luke, the disciple of Paul, wrote a Gospel (*Against Marcion* 4.5). Tertullian defends the authority of Acts of the Apostles, though without explicit attribution to Luke (*Against Heresies* 5.1).

Origen: Luke wrote the third Gospel for the Gentiles and it was praised by Paul (Eusebius's *Church History* 6.25.6). Luke wrote Acts of the Apostles (Eusebius's *Church History* 6.25.14).

Jerome: Luke was a physician from Antioch, and was highly literate in Greek. He traveled with Paul in all his journeys. Paul mentions Luke in 2 Cor 8:18; Col 4:14; and 2 Tm 4:11. He wrote a Gospel and Acts of the Apostles (*Illustrious Men* 7).

Augustine: Luke edited Matthew and Mark, and wrote third (*Consensus of the Gospels* 1.2.4). Luke wrote Acts of the Apostles (*Consensus of the Gospels* 4.8.9).

Authorship

First, we should say that Luke and The Acts of the Apostles were written by the same person. This is indicted by the first several verses of each (Lk 1:1-4, Acts 1:1), as well as the uniform style throughout. From the introduction to Luke, we know that he was not an eyewitness of Jesus. Also, he never names himself. Greek scholars agree that the author of Luke was highly educated and wrote elegantly. This translates into the English version. Whether he was a historian, a physician, both, or something else continues to be debated and will probably never be resolved without ambiguity.

We analyze the tradition for Luke much the same way that we analyzed the tradition for Mark. We know that the traditions are independent because they do not agree completely. They do all agree on the authorship, so many independent traditions point to the same answer. The traditions' source must have started before Irenaeus and Clement, so it is early. Because of this, we must accept that Luke is the author of the Gospel bearing his name, and that he was an associate of Paul. This association is given more depth by the "we passages" of Acts. Luke refers to Paul and himself as "we" four times (Acts 16:10-17, 20:5-15, 21:1-18, 27:1-28:16). We also have the references in the letters of Paul (Col 4:14; Phlm 24; 2 Tm 4:11). These passages all indicate that Luke was a close friend and traveling companion of Paul, which hangs together with the ancient tradition. Therefore, we should agree that the Luke from the New Testament is the author of Luke.

Dating

Unfortunately, like Mark, the tradition does not allow us to nail down the date of writing. Because of the four source hypothesis, we know that Luke was written after Mark (A.D. 55-70). Assuming that Mark and Luke were not in the same community, we should give Mark's Gospel some time to propagate to Luke and become a trusted document. Therefore, the earliest that Luke could reasonably have been written is about A.D. 60. For Acts, we also must take into account that Acts ends its description of events in A.D. 60. Therefore the earliest that Acts could have been written is about A.D. 65. Like Mark, the tradition disagrees about whether Luke wrote before or after the deaths of Peter and Paul. Again similar to Mark, this confusion should not have occurred if Luke wrote well after their deaths. This implies an upper limit on the date of composition to be A.D. 75 for the Gospel. Because the tradition seems to refer to the Gospel, and not to Acts, we should allow some extra time for Acts to be written and move the upper limit to A.D. 85.

The Gospel According to Matthew and Q

Summary of the Tradition

Papias: Matthew composed the sayings of the Lord in the Hebrew language, and everyone translated them as best as they could (Eusebius's *Church History* 3.39.16).

Muratorian Fragment: The fragment indicates that there are four Gospels, but the surviving text only names the Gospels of Luke and John.

Irenaeus: Matthew wrote a Gospel in the Hebrew language, while Peter and Paul were preaching the Gospel and founding the church in Rome (*Against Heresies* 3.1.1).

Clement: Matthew was written before Mark and John and at the same time as Luke (Eusebius's *Church History* 6.14.5-7).

Tertullian: Matthew wrote a Gospel (*Against Marcion* 4.5).

Origen: The first Gospel was that according to Matthew, who was once a toll-collector but later an apostle of Jesus Christ. He published it for those who became believers from Judaism, since it was composed in the Hebrew language (Eusebius's *Church History* 6.25.4).

Jerome: Matthew – who was also (called) Levi – was an apostle and former tax-collector. He first composed the Gospel of Christ in Hebrew letters and wrote for the Jews of Judea. It is not known who translated the Gospel into Greek. The Hebrew Gospel still exists, and Jerome claimed to have read it. [It is unclear whether this is an original or whether it is a translation from the Greek.] Matthew used the Hebrew Old Testament for quotes rather than the Greek one [This is not true. Current scholarship indicates that Greek Matthew used the Greek Old Testament.] (*Illustrious Men* 3)

Augustine: Matthew wrote first and gave the basic story of Jesus's life (*Consensus of the Gospels* 1.2.4).

Authorship

First, we must understand that the Gospel of Matthew heavily relies on the Gospel of Mark as a source. We get this from the four source hypothesis. Mark was not nearly as close to Jesus as Matthew, the apostle. He was an associate of Peter, not of Jesus, like Matthew. It is extremely unlikely that the apostle Matthew would quote Mark as heavily as the author of this Gospel does. He would rely on his own memories or those of others very close to Jesus. This implies that the author of Matthew is not the apostle. However, when looked at carefully, it appears that the tradition is referring to a different text, a *Hebrew* Gospel, when identifying the author. The Gospel that we now have was originally written in Greek. Also, this Hebrew Gospel of Matthew was originally identified as a sayings Gospel, which implies that it may have been a list of the teachings of Jesus, and not a full fledged story. At some time between Papias and Jerome, the church forgot that there were two different texts, a Hebrew Matthew and a Greek Matthew, and therefore identified Matthew as the author of both, even though current scholarship clearly shows that this cannot be the case.

It is commonly asserted that the Hebrew Matthew has been lost. While it is true that it no longer exists as an independent document, we must realize that its contents would not have been lost. The apostle's writings are of extremely high importance, because they are eyewitness accounts of Jesus. The early church would not have thrown them away or allowed them to be lost. However, they could have incorporated them into other writings. That is, the Hebrew Matthew has been included somewhere in the other Gospels. This is the only way that the church would not have seen the need to keep the Hebrew Matthew (quite likely not a complete Gospel) as a separate text. Now, we know that both Matthew and Luke have included within them the group of sayings known as Q. This is an early collection that we do not know the author of. Possibly, this is the Hebrew Matthew or an early translation of it. There is no other reasonable explanation that matches the facts.[12] This would also help explain how the church fathers could start saying that the Greek Matthew was written by the apostle. If the Hebrew Matthew is part of the Greek Matthew, it is not that gigantic a mistake.

Unfortunately, all this means we don't really know who the author of the Greek Matthew was. What we do know is that he was a Jewish Christian who combined Q, Mark, and some other sources together. We know that he was Jewish because he deals heavily with the place of Judaism in Christianity and quotes the Old Testament extensively.

---

12   I should mention that my identification of the author of Q with the apostle Matthew is not popular. However, even if you do not accept this, the rest of the analysis stands.

Dating

Since we are now discussing two texts, we should discuss two sets of dates. It is difficult to date either based on tradition because the church fathers do not carefully state which text they are talking about. Therefore, we must use the texts themselves and accept fairly wide ranges. We know that the Q was written before Luke (A.D. 60-75). Also, Mark (A.D. 55-70) did not use it, so it was probably not written long before Mark wrote. This allows us to date it between A.D. 45 and 70. To date the Greek Matthew, we know that it does not depend on Luke; and Luke does not depend on it; so they must have been written at about the same time. We also know that it was written after Mark and Q. Therefore, we know that it was written sometime between A.D. 60 and 85.

4.1.3 The Writings of John

The Gospel According to John

Summary of the Tradition

Papias: No comment from Papias has survived.

Muratorian Fragment: John wrote the fourth Gospel under the urging of disciples, bishops, and the apostle Andrew.

Irenaeus, student of Polycarp, student of John the apostle (Eusebius's *Church History* 5.20): John was the last Gospel written. It was written by John the apostle, while he was living in Ephesus in Asia Minor (*Against Heresies* 3.1.1). John died during the reign of Trajan (A.D. 98-117) in Ephesus (*Against Heresies* 3.3.4).

Clement: John wrote a spiritual Gospel, and was aware of the other three (Eusebius's *Church History* 6.14.5-7).

Tertullian: John wrote a Gospel (*Against Marcion* 4.5).

Origen: John wrote the last Gospel (Eusebius's *Church History* 6.25.6).

Jerome: John wrote a Gospel at the desire of the bishops of Asia. John died 68 years after the Lord's passion (*Illustrious Men* 9). The passion was in A.D. 27-34,[13] which puts John's death around A.D. 100.

Augustine: John wrote to fill in what the others had omitted (*The Harmony of the Gospels* 1.4.7).

Authorship

The tradition is unanimous from the earliest records that we have. There are some small variations in the wording and the emphasis, but there are no real contradictions. In this case, we can even trace our knowledge of the information back to John the apostle, by way of Polycarp by way of Irenaeus. This alone is enough to establish John as the author. However, we actually have more information, from the text itself. From Jn 21:20-24, we know that the curious figure of "The disciple whom Jesus loved" or "the other disciple" wrote the Gospel of John. He is mentioned several times (Jn 13:23, 18:15-16, 19:26, 20:2-8, 21:20-24). There are many clues that lead us to believe that this is John the apostle. First, we must realize that this disciple was present at the last supper and shows a very close relationship to Jesus.

> When he had said this, Jesus was deeply troubled and testified, "Amen, amen, I say to you, one of you will betray me." The disciples looked at one another, at a loss as to whom he meant. One of his disciples, the one whom Jesus loved, was reclining at Jesus's side. So Simon Peter nodded to him to find out whom he

---

13   Finegan, *Handbook of Biblical Chronology*, § 616

meant. He said to him, "Master, who is it?" Jesus answered, "It
is the one to whom I hand the morsel after I have dipped it." So
he dipped the morsel and [took it and] handed it to Judas, son of
Simon the Iscariot. (John 13:21-26)

This indicates that the title, "The disciple whom Jesus loved"
was not merely an honorific. It indicated the real relationship
between Jesus and the disciple. That means that the disciple
is one of the apostles, and probably one of the closest
apostles. Additionally Mark 14:17 (and parallels in Mt 26:20,
Lk 22:14) indicate that no one except the apostles were at the
last supper. All of the apostles are named in the Gospel of
John except for John, son of Zebedee, James, son of Zebedee,
Matthew, James, son of Alphaeus, Bartholomew, Thaddaeus,
and Simon the Zealot. From the synoptic Gospels, it is
understood that the closest apostles to Jesus are Peter and the
sons of Zebedee. For example, these three were his companions
for the vigil at Gethsemane (Mk 14:33 and parallels). The
disciple whom Jesus loved cannot be Peter, because Peter and
the disciple are mentioned together in the above passages. He
cannot reasonably be James, because James was martyred no
later than A.D. 44 (Acts 12:2). This argument from the Gospel
itself falls short of proof; but it does complement well the
tradition, which is sufficient proof by itself.

However, there is one substantial caveat. It appears that more
than one person had a hand in this Gospel. The prologue has
a different style than the rest of the Gospel. The author of
the epilogue speaks of "the disciple whom Jesus loved" in the
third person and himself in the first person. Within the Gospel,
there is some clumsiness that a single writer would have been
unlikely to create. For example, there are two endings to the
public ministry (Jn 10:40-42 and Jn 12:37-43), and two endings
for the last supper discourse of Jesus (Jn 14:31 and Jn 18:1). It
appears that the current Gospel is a combination of shorter,
homogeneous originals.

So, we have proof that John the apostle wrote the Gospel, and that the Gospel was written by more than one person. How do we resolve this apparent contradiction? We must understand that the people of this time had a slightly different definition for author than we do. When they said author, they meant the source of the tradition, not the person who actually held the pen. To know that this is a reasonable interpretation, look at Jn 19:22, "Pilate answered, 'What I have written, I have written.'" Here Pilate is saying that he wrote the inscription on Jesus's cross, but what he means is that he is responsible for the inscription. That he did not actually do the writing is clear from the previous several verses as well as the very low probability that a governor of a province would have a direct hand in the execution of a convict.

In conclusion, John is the primary source of this Gospel. He told those around him what he remembered of Jesus. It is probable that much of this was written down by his disciples while he was alive, but the Gospel was not put in its final form until after his death. Some of the clunkiness could have been smoothed out by asking him what he remembered, but he was no longer around to ask. Instead, the authors were cautious and kept the somewhat contradictory material in rather than risk losing an authentic tradition.

Dating

The tradition asserts that John lived till around A.D. 100. The Gospel's epilogue (Jn 21:23) looks to have been written around the time of John's death. Otherwise, the timing of John's death with respect to the second coming of Jesus would not have been a controversy. We can also look at papyrus fragments. C.H. Roberts discovered and published an Egyptian papyrus fragment (P^{52}) of John chapter 18 that is dated between A.D. 135 and 150. There are also two long papyri texts of John from the end of the second century in the Bodmer collection ($P^{60,75}$). You may ask where these dates come from. Experts study the handwriting and compare it to standard texts with non-disputable dates. This has become a universal and well accepted method of dating ancient manuscripts. The fancy description of this technique is paleographic dating. These dates are later, but it gives supporting evidence that a date near the death of John is reasonable.

Using John's death as a fixed point, it is likely that the Gospel was completed between A.D. 95 and 115. As discussed in the authorship section, this Gospel had a drawn out creation process, so much of it was written earlier, possibly much earlier.

The Letters of John

Summary of the Tradition

Polycarp: The first letter is quoted, but without attribution *(Epistle to the Philippians* 7).

Papias: Eusebius indicates *(Church History* 3.39.16) that Papias relies on the first letter of John, but Papias's actual words have been lost. Regarding the other letters, Jerome regarded Papias' following comment relevant:

> If, then, any one who had attended on the elders came, I asked minutely after their sayings - what Andrew or Peter said, or what was said by Philip, or by Thomas, or by James, or by John, or by Matthew, or by any other of the Lord's disciples: which things Aristion and the presbyter John, the disciples of the Lord, say. (Jerome's *Lives of Illustrious Men* 18)

This indicates the possibility of two different Johns, an apostle John, and a presbyter (elder) John. However, Papias does not mention the other letters in his surviving fragments.

Muratorian Fragment: There are at least two letters written by John, and the first letter is quoted.

Irenaeus: The first letter is quoted, with attribution to John (*Against Heresies* 3.16.5). The second letter is also quoted, with attribution to John (*Against Heresies* 1.16.3). The third letter is not mentioned.

Clement: The first letter is quoted, with attribution to John the apostle (*Stromata* 2.15). He quotes it as being the longer letter, but he does not quote the other letters in the surviving texts.

Tertullian: Tertullian quotes the first letter frequently, with John as the author (*Against Marcion* 5.16, *Against Praxeas* 15, 28, *Scorpiace* 12 and others).

Origen: Origen frequently quotes John at the author of the first letter (*Commentary on the Gospel of John* 6.26 and others). He states that it is unknown if the second and third letters are genuine (Eusebius's *Church History* 6.25.10).

Jerome: John the apostle wrote the first letter. John the elder wrote the other two. He bases this on the quotation of Papias, above (*Illustrious Men* 9).

Augustine: Augustine wrote *Homilies on the First Epistle of John*, with John listed as the author. He states that there are three letters of John (*On Christian Doctrine* 2.8.13).

Authorship

All of the letters and the Gospel share common themes and word choices, quickly implying to a casual inspection that they are all from the same community of believers. This impression becomes stronger as the text is analyzed more thoroughly, in word choices, style, theological emphasis, and many direct cross references. At minimum then, the letters and the Gospel are all from the Johannine community. This community may be defined more through shared relationships and history than geography, however.

For the first letter of John, the tradition is unanimous and goes back to the beginning. Unlike for the Gospel, there is no real evidence of multiple authors. In addition, in the introduction (1 Jn 1:1-4), the unnamed author indicates that he is a direct eye witness. The author speaks with an unmistakable air of authority. Finally, he refers to his target audience as dear children as would be expected of the now old John the Apostle. For these reasons, ascribing this letter directly to John is the most reasonable action. However, when we discuss the Apocalypse, we will assert that it was probably written by John as well, even though the Greek is much worse. This implies that this letter was likely written with the assistance of an amanuensis (personal secretary).

The evidence is much thinner for the other two letters. The letters themselves are very short. While the first letter is a developed sermon, the other two are personal letters that conclude with a promise to visit, so that more can be discussed. This makes textual criticism difficult, except to say that the second two letters are written by the same person (the self-identified presbyter of 2 Jn 1:1; 3 Jn 1:1) due to the nearly identical format.

The short length of the letters undoubtedly is the reason that these two letters were referenced so rarely in the tradition. We only have one solid ancient witness (Irenaeus) on which to base authorship, and several incidental references. Jerome's evidence that the apostle and the presbyter were not the same person and that Papias was referring to the author of the letters is not convincing. By default, then, we should identify the author of the second and third letters as John, but the evidence is admittedly weak. If he is not the author, then it is certainly a member of the Johannine community.

Dating

Precise dating of the letters is difficult. It would be tricky to understand the letters without the Gospel, which implies that the Gospel already existed; but it is clearly possible that the Gospel existed only in oral form when the letters were written. Note that the presbyter of the second and third letters indicates a substantial oral preference. "Although I have much to write to you, I do not intend to use paper and ink. Instead, I hope to visit you and to speak face to face so that our joy may be complete" (2 Jn 12; 3 Jn 13-14). The first letter was written by John when he was old (but not dead), so we can expect that it was written between A.D. 60 and 100. We have even less to go on for the second and third letters. From the topics of the letters, we know that the church already had multiple communities and disputes, so an extremely early date is unlikely. However, Paul's letter to the Galatians from the early 50's (§ 4.1.4) also indicates multiple communities and doctrinal disputes. A very late date is impossible because Irenaeus quotes the second letter as authoritative and from before his time. The nearly identical formats of the second and third letters make it likely that they were not only written by the same person, but also at about the same time. This analysis gives a wide range of A.D. 45-130. If we accept authorship by John, then we can move the end date to A.D. 100.

The Apocalypse

Summary of the Tradition

Justin Martyr (A.D. ca. 114-165): John the apostle prophesied the revelation (*Dialog with Trypho* 81).

Muratorian Fragment: The fragment includes the Apocalypse as having been written by John.

Irenaeus: The apocalypse was seen towards the end of Domitian's reign, by John (*Against Heresies*, 5.30). He is not labeled as the apostle in this passage, but Irenaeus frequently refers to John the apostle elsewhere, and no other Johns. Domitian was put to death in A.D. 96.

Clement: John went to Ephesus after Patmos (*Who is the rich man that shall be saved* 42).

Tertullian: John the apostle (*Against Marcion* 4.2) is the author (*Against Marcion* 4.5).

Origen: Origen identifies the author of the Apocalypse as John the apostle (*Commentary on the Gospel of John,* 2.4).

Dionysius of Alexandria (A.D. ca. 190-265): Based on style and the differences in writing ability, the authors of the Gospel and the Apocalypse cannot be the same person (Eusebius's *Church History* 7.25.7).

Victorinus (died A.D. ca. 303): John saw the Apocalypse while at Patmos, and delivered it after Domitian's death and John's release (*Commentary on the Apocalypse of the Blessed John* 10.11).

Eusebius: quotes Justin as confirming that John the apostle was the author (*Church History* 4.18.8), and quotes Irenaeus as indicating that the apostle John wrote the Apocalypse during the end of Domitian's reign, from the island of Patmos. States that others do not accept it (*Church History* 3.25.1-7), including Dionysius *(Church History* 7.25.7). Eusebius himself does not commit to a conclusion regarding authorship (*Church History* 3.25.2, 3.39.6).

Cyril of Jerusalem (A.D. ca. 315 - ca. 386): Does not list the Apocalypse in his canon (*Catechetical Lectures* 4.36).

Gregory of Nazianzus (A.D. ca. 329 - ca. 389): Does not list the Apocalypse in his canon (*Carmina Dogmatica* 1.1).

Jerome:

> In the fourteenth year then after Nero, Domitian, having raised a second persecution, he (John the apostle) was banished to the island of Patmos, and wrote the Apocalypse, on which Justin Martyr and Irenaeus afterwards wrote commentaries. But Domitian having been put to death and his acts, on account of his excessive cruelty, having been annulled by the senate, he returned to Ephesus under Pertinax and continuing there until the tithe of the emperor Trajan, founded and built churches throughout all Asia, and, worn out by old age, died in the sixty-eighth year after our Lord's passion and was buried near the same city (*Lives of Illustrious Men* 9).

> John is both an Apostle and an Evangelist, and a prophet. An Apostle, because he wrote to the Churches as a master; an Evangelist, because he composed a Gospel, a thing which no other of the Apostles, excepting Matthew, did; a prophet, for he saw in the island of Patmos, to which he had been banished by the Emperor Domitian as a martyr for the Lord, an Apocalypse containing the boundless mysteries of the future (*Against Jovinianus* 1).

Augustine: Augustine includes the Apocalypse in his canon (*On Christian Doctrine* 2.8.13).

Authorship

In the Apocalypse, the author self identifies as John, who was exiled to Patmos, a prison colony, because of his witness to the faith (Rev 1:9). He does not identify himself as the apostle, but he does not say that he is not the apostle, either. With respect to the tradition, there are two schools of thought among the church fathers. The western fathers, of which Irenaeus is the most important witness, assert that John the apostle is the author, and that he wrote the Apocalypse while at the prison colony of Patmos. Irenaeus is identified as the source of the written tradition because he is very early, and because he can claim authority as being a student of Polycarp, who was a student of John (Eusebius's *Church History* 5.20). The eastern fathers, however, of which Dionysius is the most important witness, reject the authenticity of the Apocalypse. Dionysius rejected it because the Greek of the Apocalypse is very poor when compared to the other documents attributed to John. This argument still holds weight today, but note that Dionysius apparently had no access to the Johannine community, but only the texts. In many ways he was the first practitioner of biblical textual criticism. He is also one of the most successful, as his understanding that the Apocalypse and the Gospel were written by different people is still agreed with today. In addition, the eastern fathers may have rejected the Apocalypse because a literal reading can lead to some problematic teachings, especially on the topic of Millenialism (Rev 20:1-7). Current Catholic understanding, which goes back at least to Eusebius (*Church History* 3.39.12), is that the Apocalypse should be read symbolically.

On one hand, we have Irenaeus, who was close enough to the people involved to have the correct understanding of authorship and affirmed John as the author, while on the other hand, we have the clear textual evidence that the documents were not written by the same person. To resolve this contradiction, we must remember our understanding that the Gospel was not actually written by John, but by one (or more) of his assistants; and in the ancient world, the author was the one who stood behind the document, not the one who held the pen. In this way, we have five documents: the Gospel, the three letters, and the Apocalypse, of which are all were written by John in spirit, but written by others in mechanics. Of these, the Apocalypse is the most likely to have actually been written by John because he wrote it from prison, and would be less likely to have assistance. If he did have an assistant, that assistant should be fired, as the Greek of the Apocalypse is poor. Note that John, as a Jewish fisherman, would be expected to have poor ability in written Greek.

Dating

There is no good reason to deny the tradition that it was written around A.D. 90-95, at the end of the Domitian persecution. The attestation is old and consistent. Attempts to place it earlier, during Nero's time, rely on specific interpretations of the Apocalypse. Gathering historical information from the symbolic language of the Apocalypse is dubious at best.

4.1.4 The Letters of Paul

Paul was a strict Pharisee and a primary persecutor of Christians soon after Jesus's death. After Paul had been doing this for some time, Jesus came to him in a vision (Acts 9:1-28), and Paul converted to Christianity. He spent the rest of his life as a traveling missionary, spreading the gospel (good news) to the world; and his letters were part of this. Because of his writings, we know more about him than any other person mentioned in the New Testament; but there are still notable gaps. Paul did not intend these letters to be kept for posterity. He wrote them to communicate with distant churches, to encourage, to cajole, to inform, and to respond to events that he had heard about. The reason they have been kept is because they are full of timeless wisdom, as well as being the earliest writings of the Christian church.

Authorship

Paul lists himself as the author of each of his letters. From the earliest references we have (early second century) until relatively recent times (nineteenth century), all of these letters were accepted as written by Paul. The external attestation is both wide (many sources) and ancient. Therefore, using arguments from tradition like those we used for the Gospels, there is no reason to doubt Paul's authorship. However, because of the popularity of the arguments, we must discuss why doubt is cast on some of Paul's letters. What follows is an outline only. To get the complete arguments, and if you have a lot of time on your hands, read the relevant sections of Donald Guthrie, *New Testament Introduction*, which defends Pauline authorship and/or Raymond E. Brown, *An Introduction to the New Testament*, which accepts Pauline authorship on some letters, but not others. Both introductions attempt to describe both sides of every argument.

The following kinds of arguments are used to disparage Pauline authorship:
Stylistic: The author uses different vocabulary and grammar in a not-trusted set of letters verses a trusted set of letters.

Theological: The theology of one letter is not that consistent the theology of another. The author uses theological terms differently or emphasizes different points.

Excessive Similarities: One letter has very similar wording to another, except that parts have been added or removed. That is, someone copied a letter but changed it to meet his needs.

Not Corroborated by Acts: Paul describes events that do not appear in Acts.

Anachronisms: Concepts are discussed and heresies are argued against that could not have been issues in Paul's time.

Counter-arguments:
Because the argument from tradition is so strong, arguments against Pauline authorship should only be accepted if they are overwhelming. They are not. In every case, we can give reasons

for how Paul could have written the letter in question, in spite of the objections.

Stylistic: When writing a different letter, Paul was writing on a different topic, in a different emotional state, to a different audience, and at a different stage in his life. Each of these will cause stylistic changes of varying degrees that are very difficult to quantify. Any stylistic argument is therefore a very subjective one. Also, it is quite possible that Paul used an amanuensis (personal secretary). This amanuensis could have had some freedom to write in his own words, while working under the direction of Paul. Before the days of e-mail, this sort of arrangement was common. The author would still be considered Paul, because he decides the actual content and themes of the letter, though not necessarily every word.

Theological: It is plausible that Paul could use words in different ways in different contexts. For example, he can speak of faith as belief in Jesus, or he can speak of "the faith" as the complete tradition about Jesus, which must be handed down to the next generation. It is also plausible that he decided to emphasize one theological point in one letter, but a different point in another, because of the different circumstances under which the letter was written.

Excessive Similarities: Paul spoke and wrote on the same themes often, to many different audiences. It would not be surprising if the same wording came out from time to time, but with changes to match the different circumstances. Paul (or an amanuensis) may even have kept copies of his old letters, so that he did not have to start from scratch every time.

Not Corroborated by Acts: These arguments generally rely on the assumption that Acts is a complete record of Paul's life. However, this is just not the case. Most especially, Acts ends with Paul's imprisonment in Rome, from A.D. 58 to 60 (see below), while he was not martyred until A.D. 67. A lot could have happened in these seven years, and the events that Paul refers to could have come from this time. It is also possible that Luke left some events out from before A.D. 58.

Anachronisms: Arguments along these lines are extremely subjective, because they require that we understand exactly when certain theological or ecclesiastical concepts became common in the years after Jesus, which is difficult because of the relatively small number of writings that we have. Also, note that by the time of Paul's death, about thirty-five years had passed since the crucifixion of Jesus. It would not be shocking if certain concepts, both heretical and orthodox, had progressed quite far by then.

Chronology of Paul's Life

From Acts, Paul's letters, and tradition it is possible to date Paul's life to fairly high accuracy. *The Handbook of Biblical Chronology*, § 673-698, by Jack Finegan gives a systematic exposition of these dates. A summary follows. Most of the dates are trustworthy to within a few years. Luke recorded how long Paul was at most of his stops, but he usually does not record how long it took Paul to travel from one point to another, and this leads to some small uncertainty. Also, some of the lengths of time that Luke gives may be approximate. Finally, there are some events for which the ordering is not certain, such as the Jerusalem conference, because of the thinness of the record for those events.

A.D. 33: Jesus is crucified (Finegan, § 620).

A.D. 36: Paul is converted (Acts 9:1-30), 14 years before the Jerusalem conference (Gal 2:1).

A.D. 38: Paul visits Jerusalem, three years after his conversion (Gal 1:18).

A.D. 38-47: Paul evangelizes in Syria and Cilicia (Gal 1:21) and possibly other regions. The record on these years is thin.

A.D. 47-48: Paul completes his first missionary journey (Acts 13-14).

Early A.D. 49: Paul attends the Jerusalem conference (Acts 15:1-29, Gal 2:2-10).

Spring, A.D. 49 - fall A.D. 49: Paul begins his second missionary journey (Acts 15:30-17:34).

Winter, A.D. 49/50 - early summer, A.D. 51: Paul stays in Corinth for a year and a half (Acts 18:1-11).

Early summer, A.D. 51: Paul is brought before Proconsul Gallio (Acts 18:12-18:17). This is the primary fixed point in Paul's life, because it is the date that has the most narrow constraint on when it happened. We know this because of an inscription (found in Delphi in pieces from A.D. 1885-1910) with the date of Gallio's proconsulate, and we know the proconsuls had one year terms.

Late summer and fall, A.D. 51: Paul completes his second missionary journey (Acts 18:18-21).

Winter, A.D. 51/52: Paul winters in Antioch (Acts 18:22-23).

Spring, A.D. 52: Paul begins his third missionary journey (Acts 18:23-19:1).

Summer, A.D. 52 - fall, A.D. 54: Paul spends two years and three months in the Ephesus (Acts 19).

Fall, A.D. 54 - spring A.D. 55: Paul completes the third missionary journey and arrives in Jerusalem (Acts 20-21).

Summer, A.D. 55 - summer, A.D. 57: Paul is arrested in Jerusalem (Acts 21:33) and transferred to Caesarea (Acts 23:33) under the control of the governor Felix. After two years, Felix is succeeded by Porcius Festus.

Summer, A.D. 57 - fall, A.D. 57: Paul stands before Festus and King Agrippa II, and appeals to Caesar (Acts 24-26), using his rights as a Roman citizen. This means that he would be tried in Rome instead of Caesarea. Paul is sent on his way to Rome by ship. They were blown off course by a storm and ship wrecked on Malta (Acts 27).

Winter, A.D. 57/58: Paul winters on Malta (Acts 28:1-10).

Winter, A.D. 58 - winter A.D. 60: Paul completes the journey to Rome. He stays there under house arrest, for two years (Acts 28:11-30). Acts ends, so the record becomes thin and less reliable at this point.

Winter, A.D. 60-67: According to Eusebius (*Church History* 2.22.2), Paul is released after two years in prison and continues his missionary work. We know that he had planned to go to Spain (Rom 15:24, 28). There are references by Clement of Rome (1 Clement 5) and the Muratorian Fragment that Paul did make this trip. Paul's letters to Timothy and Titus indicate that he made it back to Greece after visiting Spain. It is impossible to prove that this Spanish trip did or did not happen because of the thinness of the record. Afterward, he was martyred with Peter under Nero, on June 29th, A.D. 67 (Finegan, § 670-673).

Dating the Letters

It is likely that Paul did not write many letters until the beginning of his second missionary journey in A.D. 49. There would not be much point in writing letters until he was already somewhat well traveled, and had people to write to. The oldest letter that we have is 1 Thessalonians, and it was written around A.D. 49-51. He continued writing letters up until his death in A.D. 67, so we have a range of A.D. 49-67 for all of his letters. Attempting to date the letters more accurately is like putting together an intricate puzzle that is missing many of the pieces. Some letters can be dated fairly precisely, such as 1 Thessalonians, and others not so much. I give the most probable dates of the letters below. Because of the arguments' length, their peripheral relevance to this book, and their tendency to put people to sleep, I do not put them here, but only give a very brief outline. For the full arguments, see the introductions mentioned above. They give slightly different dates, because they did not use Finegan as the source for the chronology of Paul's life.

1 Thessalonians A.D. 49-51:
Dating is based on traveling companions and cross references between 1 Thessalonians and Acts.

Galatians A.D. 49-54:
Dating is based on when Paul visited Galatia and his anger at them for having quickly forsaken his teachings (Gal 1:6-9). This is complicated because there are two possible definitions for Galatia. That is, did he mean the Roman province or the region where the ethnic Galations lived?

2 Thessalonians A.D. 52-54:
Based on the themes of the letter, it was likely written after 1 Thessalonians and before Paul's next visit to Thessalonica (in Macedonia) in A.D. 54.

1 Corinthians A.D. 52-54:
Paul wrote from Ephesus (1 Cor 16:8), probably during the lengthy visit from A.D. 52-54.

Romans A.D. 54-55:
Dating is based on persons' names and cross references with 1 Corinthians and Acts.

2 Corinthians A.D. 55:
This letter was written after 1 Corinthians, based on the internal references and logical consistency between 1 and 2 Corinthians. It is likely that 2 Corinthians is actually several letters, combined together, which complicates the issue. Because he had not yet been in prison, these letters were completed before his Caesarean imprisonment, which began in A.D. 56.

Philippians A.D. 58-60:
This is one of the four captivity epistles (Phil 1:7,13,17). Generally, the imprisonment in Rome is considered the most probable (A.D. 58-60) for all of the captivity epistles. This is the traditional answer, and there is also a lot of internal evidence that suggests that this is indeed the case. However, the case is not airtight, so it is possible that some or all of the captivity epistles were written during some other imprisonment at some other time.

Colossians A.D. 58-60:
This is one of the four captivity epistles (Col 4:18).

Philemon A.D. 58-60:
This is one of the four captivity epistles (Phlm 9).

Ephesians A.D. 58-60:
This is one of the four captivity epistles (Eph 4:1).

1 Timothy A.D. 62-67:
1 Timothy indicates events that have occurred after Acts, including substantial traveling. Allowing time for this traveling puts a minimum date of 62. The upper limit is his death in 67.

Titus A.D. 62-67:
The evidence here is the same as for 1 Timothy.

2 Timothy A.D. 67:
Paul indicates that he is about to be martyred, so it was likely written in 67. If his premonition is false, it would have been written earlier, but certainly after 62, for the same reasons as 1 Timothy and Titus.

4.1.5 The Other Letters

The Letter of James

The author lists himself as "James, a slave of God and of the Lord Jesus Christ" (Jas 1:1). This James is unlikely to be the son of Zebedee, as that James was martyred in A.D. 44 and there is no evidence for a very early date for the letter. Most commonly, the author has been believed to be James, the brother of Jesus (Mt 13:55; Mk 6:3; Acts 1:14; 1 Cor 15:7). This is supported by parallels between the letter of James and the speech of James in Acts 15. James was a common name during this time, and there are several others in the New Testament, so some other James is still a possibility. The support from tradition is weak on this letter. Origen refers to it (*Commentary on John* 19.61), as do Eusebius (*Church History* 2.23.25), and Jerome (*Illustrious Men* 2). However, both Eusebius and Jerome list the letter as being disputed by some. Taken together, it is difficult to be sure which James wrote it. The Greek of the letter is very good, making it likely that an amanuensis assisted with the writing. James, the brother of Jesus, was martyred in A.D. 61, so if we accept his authorship, it was likely written in the 50s. If we don't, it was probably written later, but most likely before A.D. 100, as a late date would have made it easier to identify as a forgery to the church fathers, and there is no internal evidence of a late date.

The Letter of Jude

The author self-identifies as "Jude, a slave of Jesus Christ and brother of James" (Jude 1). This is generally understood to make him Jude, the brother of James and Jesus (Mk 6:3, Mt 13:55). The Muratorian Fragment, Clement (*Stromata* 3.2.11), and Tertullian (*On Female Fashion* 1.3) accept it. Origen (*Commentary on Matthew* 10.17) also accepts it, but states that not all do (*Commentary on John* 19.6). Eusebius lists it as disputed (*Church History* 3.25.3), and Jerome accepted it (*Letter to Paulinus* 9). Many of the fathers never mention it. However, it is likely that those who rejected it, rejected it because of its content rather than its source. It is short and not that useful. In addition, it quotes two non-canonical and not particularly reputable sources: *The Assumption of Moses* (Jude 9) and *Enoch* 1 (Jude 14-15). The weight of the evidence is on the side of the letter being authentic, but the evidence is on the light side. If it was indeed written by Jude, the brother of James, a date between A.D. 60 and 100 is reasonable. If not written by Jude, we should increase the range to A.D. 120. A much later date is unlikely, because we have early sources that label the letter as authentic.

First Letter of Peter

The author claims to be the apostle Peter (1 Pet 1:1) and is confirmed as such by all the church fathers who comment. It is quoted without attribution by Polycarp (*Letter to the Philippians* 8.1 and others) and Tertullian (*Scorpiace* 12). It is quoted with attribution by Irenaeus (*Against Heresies* 5.7.2) and Clement (Eusebius's *Church History* 2.15.2). Authorship is confirmed by Origen (Eusebius's *Church History* 6.25.8) and Jerome (*Illustrious Men* 1). In this way the situation is similar with the letters of Paul, in that the default position is to accept authenticity unless there is overwhelming evidence to the contrary. The objections to authentic authorship are recent and similar to those used against Paul. The first objection is that the Greek is highly polished and unlikely to come from a Galilean fisherman. However, in the conclusion he writes "I write you this briefly through Silvanus, whom I consider a faithful brother" (1 Pet 5:12). This implies that Silvanus is the amanuensis for this letter. Another objection is that the persecutions described by Peter in the letter must refer to the more widespread persecutions of Domitian or Trajan after Peter's death. However, even if the persecutions had not yet reached the eastern churches (the addressee of Peter's letter) it would be reasonable for Peter to assume that because persecution was rampant in Rome, that it was a problem elsewhere as well. Finally, objections are raised that Peter's writing is too similar to Paul's; but this requires very specific and unjustified assumptions about the relationship between Peter and Paul. Because of the emphasis on persecution (1 Pet 4:12-19) it is likely that the letter was written during Nero's persecution of Christianity towards the end of his reign. This would place the letter somewhere from A.D. 64-67. Nero's persecution led to Peter's execution in A.D. 67 in Rome.

Second Letter of Peter

The second letter is in a very different category than the first. Specifically, few of the church fathers refer to it; and those that do refer to it, use it with reservations. Origen (Eusebius's *Church History* 6.25.8), Jerome (*Illustrious Men* 1), and Eusebius (*Church History* 3.25.3) list it as disputed. By the time of Augustine (*On Christian Doctrine* 2.8.13), the letter began to be accepted; but this development is too late to be used to authenticate it. The author claims to be the apostle Peter (2 Peter 1:1); but he tries too hard, with explicit references to the Peter of the Gospels (2 Peter 1:16-18) and the Peter of the first letter (2 Peter 3:1). He argues against those who see the delay of the Apocalypse as a sign against Christianity (2 Peter 3). However, this would not have been an issue while Peter was still alive. The author speaks of Paul's letters as if they are already collected and part of scripture (2 Peter 3:15-16). It would be very surprising if Paul's writings had been collected and considered scripture before the deaths of Peter and Paul in A.D. 67. Because the letter is not written by Peter, an early date is unlikely. The upper limit for the letter is the writing of the Apocalypse of Peter, an apocryphal work which quotes this letter. This apocalypse is itself referred to in the Muratorian Fragment (A.D. 170). This gives the second letter of Peter a range of approximately A.D. 100-150.

The Letter to the Hebrews

The author of this letter (or more accurately, sermon) does not identify himself. Because of his focus on the relationship between Judaism and Jesus, we can be confident that he was a Jewish Christian. There have been numerous theories as to the authorship in ancient and recent times, but none of them have enough evidence to support any sort of confidence. Clement of Rome cites it in his *Letter to the Corinthians* (Compare Heb 11:37 with 1 Clem 17 and Heb 1:3-4 with 1 Clem 36); so we can date it before this letter, which is generally accepted to have been written about A.D. 95. In addition, the author refers to the rituals in the temple in the present tense, implying that they are on-going (Heb 9:6, 9:13, 13:10). This implies that the letter was written before the destruction of the temple in A.D. 70. If for some reason this use of language is a literary device (as is implied by some later documents which describe temple rites in the present tense), it would still be very odd that a letter so concerned with Jewish rituals would leave out a mention of the destruction of the temple had it already occurred. A very early date is not likely because he is not an eyewitness (Heb 2:3), and his readers have been believers for some time (Heb 5:12, 10:32). Therefore, we expect a date in the range of A.D. 60-70.

We now know that the entire New Testament was written by first-, second-, and third-hand witnesses, in the range of 20-120 years after the death of Jesus. The majority of the New Testament was written by second-hand witnesses from 30-55 years after the death of Jesus. This is a critical piece upon which the reliability of the New Testament rests. For the most part, later sections will rely on the Gospels because this is where almost all the sayings and actions of Jesus are, and Acts, because it focuses on the early history of the church. I included discussions of the letters because they give context and support to the Gospels, as well as demonstrate that Christianity existed as a movement by A.D. 50.

4.2 Reliability[14]

I strongly urge you to read a substantial amount of the New Testament. By far, the strongest argument for the authenticity of the New Testament is the New Testament itself. For the most part, my arguments below merely highlight this or that passage from the text. Assuming that you are a skeptic, you should start with Luke and Acts, which were written by the same person. You should then read Romans and Corinthians by Paul. These writings are the easiest for non-Christians to read and understand. After you read those, the order that you read in is less important.

---

14   The arguments in this section borrow heavily from Kreeft and Tacelli, *Handbook of Christian Apologetics*, Chapter 8. That chapter deals mainly with the resurrection, but the arguments pertain to the New Testament as a whole.

4.2.1 Wrote History, Not Fiction or Myth

Some people would assert that the New Testament is a fictional or mythical work. Christ did not exist; or if he did, he did not rise from the dead. The writers of the New Testament knew this, and the writing has been misinterpreted ever since. The writers were not dishonest, but they did not realize that people would blow the story way out of proportion.

This standpoint does not hold water because it does not agree with the actual writings. Regardless of whether or not Christianity is true, the authors of the New Testament want us to believe that it is. Here are some explicit examples. The first is the introduction to Luke.

> I too have decided, after investigating everything accurately anew, to write it down in an orderly sequence for you, most excellent Theophilus [friend of God], so that you may realize the certainty of the teachings you have received. (Lk 1:3-4)

Here, Luke is explicitly claiming that he is writing history. There is no other reasonable way to interpret this line.

The second example is Paul's letter to the Romans (Rom 1:1-7). Paul makes an explicit summary of the critical events of the Gospel, including the resurrection. If the Gospel is just a teaching story, it would have a much less prominent place in this letter. However, it is clear from the location of the summary that the events are the most important topic in the letter. Without the events, the letter would not have much reason to be written.

Also, when you read the Gospels, they read as realistic renditions of what occurred. In many places, there are descriptions and events that are not necessary. The only real reason to put them in is because they happened.

After Jesus is arrested, an unknown young man is following them, wearing nothing but a linen cloth (Mk 14:43-52). They seize him, but he left the cloth behind and ran off naked. The young man is not named. Why would the author include this unless he or his source knew that it happened? This line has an intimate eyewitness feel to it. It is not central to the storyline, but it is the sort of color that an eyewitness would remember.

After a crowd asks him what should be done with an adulterous woman, Jesus writes in the dirt like he is thinking and stalling for time (Jn 8:1-10). The Gospel does not say what he is writing. It is not clear whether the writing is important or not. Jesus's point "Let the one among you who is without sin be the first to throw a stone at her," does not depend on whether or not he wrote in the ground. The only reason to include this is that it actually happened.

Finally, the Gospels lack mythical hyperbole. Myths are not afraid to blow everything out of proportion. In the Gospels there are many miracles, but they happen in a matter of fact fashion. Angels don't swoop in to fancy pyrotechnic displays. They just appear or are calmly sitting down. When Lazarus is raised from the dead (Jn 11:1-44), nothing is more striking than how understated the description is. If this was myth, we should expect this event to have a lot more elaborate imagery, which was the special effects of those days. A man is getting raised from the dead, after all.[15]

So now we know that the authors of the New Testament wanted us to believe that what they wrote actually occurred. Therefore, it did occur, they were mistaken, or they were liars. Let us look at these other possibilities.

4.2.2 Not Liars[16]

Next, we consider the possibility that the authors knew the true story, and intended for the work to be received as history,

15   To see this point argued by a master, see "Modern Theology and Biblical Criticism," by C.S. Lewis. This essay is available in *Christian Reflections* and *Fern-Seed and the Elephants*.
16   This section borrows heavily from the work of Kevin King (http://life.liegeman.org/historymaker/charact.html).

but were liars. There are two key problems with this position. The first is that the writers are spreading the words and actions of Jesus, and it is impossible to image the Jesus of the New Testament (§ 5.1.4) approving of such a fabrication. You cannot serve Jesus (whether he is real or imaginary) by lying in his name.

Second, almost all of the authors of the New Testament were martyred. Those who survived had no reasonable expectation that they would survive. Why would they die for something that they themselves did not believe in? If they knew that there was no reward in heaven for their actions, martyrdom is positively irrational. We have record of disciple after disciple remaining defiant till the end.

The authors believed what they wrote to be true. We now only have two possibilities. Either the New Testament is the work of honest observers of real events or the authors, honest men though they were, were deceived or mistaken.

4.2.3 Not Deceived or Mistaken

There are some questions we must ask to determine if the authors were mistaken. Once we complete the questions, it will not be reasonable to say that the authors were mistaken.

How Close Were the Authors to the Actual Events?

The vast majority of the New Testament was written in the second half of the first century. It was complete by A.D. 150. Only a few of the authors were eyewitnesses, but the story can always be traced back to the eyewitnesses.

Is This Close Enough to Consider These Accounts Reliable?

The answer is yes. The eyewitnesses had to pass on the story before they died, of course. The eyewitnesses would not garble the story in a way that destroys the critical themes and events of the story. When you are seventy, do you forget why you married your spouse? Remember that Jesus was the most important thing that happened to them. They would be more likely to forget their love of their spouses than they would be to forget the words and deeds of their Lord. Now, that is not to say that they never made a mistake. I know that my parents argue about the details of conversations from two months ago, let alone forty years ago. Also, it is possible that they might occasionally disagree about something important from when they were young.

The situation is similar for second and third generation Christian authors. They finished writing by A.D. 150. Even though they did not see the most important event of their lives directly, it was still the most important event of their lives. It radically changed who and what they were when they learned of Jesus. They then devoted their lives to learning about Jesus and writing about him. They also had the entire Christian community to guide them. Because they were writing very soon after the events, the apostles and the apostles' immediate followers were still around to correct them. Again, it is expected that details may get altered in translation.

So, the question becomes, how do we know when the account is reliable? There are two requirements. The first is that the event must have been important. People tend to forget things that were not important at the time, so it would not be surprising if there were some mistakes here. All of contradictions in the New Testament that I know about are in the not important category. The second is that the event should be consistent with the person of Jesus from the rest of the New Testament. It is reasonably possible for two people to disagree about an old, but important, event; but if three or four agree, it is highly unlikely that the event is misconstrued in a meaningful way. Even if there is only one source on an event or saying, if that event or saying agrees with the person of Jesus found elsewhere in the New Testament, there is no good reason to disbelieve it.

In conclusion, the authors were men who indirectly witnessed extraordinary events that dramatically changed their lives and the world. It was the events that made the men, and not the men that made the events. There is no room for these men to be deceived about the events because of their closeness to them and because of how deeply they were affected by them.

Are There Other Sources That Were Equally Close or Closer That Give a Contradictory Account?

There are contradictory sources. Most of these are referred to as Gnostics. Dating these tends to be more difficult, because none of the church fathers support their authenticity. In some cases, we can say that they were written before a certain date, because a specific text is disparaged by a specific church father. Many of them were written within two centuries of Jesus's life, so they are early enough that we cannot throw them out immediately.

Are the Contradictory Accounts More Believable?

The reason that I don't expect to ever study these writings in detail is that they fail the tests that the canonical New Testament pass. The gnostic accounts are simply not believable, which is the primary reason that they did not get accepted into the New Testament. It is readily apparent when you read these alternate Gospels that the authors are writing myth, are liars, or are being deceived. To give one example, there is the Gospel of Peter. It was probably written around A.D. 125, but some believe that it was written earlier. To quote William Lane Craig:

> In this account, the tomb is not only surrounded by Roman guards but also by all the Jewish Pharisees and elders as well as a great multitude from all the surrounding countryside who have come to watch the resurrection. Suddenly in the night there rings out a loud voice in heaven, and two men descend from heaven to the tomb. The stone over the door rolls back by itself, and they go into the tomb. The three men come out of the tomb, two of them holding

up the third man. The heads of the two men reach up into the clouds, but the head of the third man reaches beyond the clouds. Then a cross comes out of the tomb, and a voice from heaven asks, "Have you preached to them that sleep?" And the cross answers, "Yes." (*Apologetics: An Introduction* p. 189)

Just like the strongest defense for the New Testament is the New Testament, the strongest argument against the alternate Gospels is the text itself. This passage has all the characteristics of a legend. It is fanciful and not believable. The other alternate Gospels are similar, to greater or lesser degrees. To a large extent, the tests I've given to prove the New Testament reliable are the same ones that the church fathers used to determine the canon, so it is not surprising that we get the same result.

We now know that the authors were writing about historical events, were not liars, and were not mistaken. Therefore, we should trust the authors just as we would trust anyone else with the same qualifications. Before I leave this section and discuss Christian doctrines that can be found in the Bible, I will discuss the topic of contradictions.

How to Deal with Contradictions

Atheists will often find hundreds of contradictions in the Bible, and then will proceed to state that this renders the Bible invalid and false. Fundamentalists will find zero contradictions and consider this to be a proof of divine authorship. How can two groups of people find such a different result when presented with the same Bible? The reason is that they are using a different method of determining whether or not there are contradictions, even though they seem to agree on what contradictions mean. That is, they agree that no contradictions make the Bible divine and true and contradictions makes the Bible false. Therefore, atheists and fundamentalists will expend a huge amount of energy debating this or that contradiction.

An atheist will call something a contradiction if a resolution is not immediately obvious to the casual observer. The atheist then declares both statements false. The first fallacy is that just because something contradicts at first impression does not mean that a more careful analysis of the data will give a contradiction. Secondly, if two things contradict, there are actually two possibilities. Either both false *or* one of them is true.

A fundamentalist will say that the contradiction can be removed by some (often drastic) stretching of our understanding of the two passages. A fundamentalist will then state that the inability to find a contradiction is another proof of divine authorship. The first fallacy is that people can be endlessly inventive. It is amazing what contradictions can be removed by enough creative rethinking of the data. The second fallacy is that just because two things are consistent, it does not prove (or really even imply) that they are both true. They could easily both be false.

The described methodologies of atheists and fundamentalists are ridiculous and would never be thought of value regarding any non-Biblical inquiry. Instead, we must answer two questions: "How do we know when there is a contradiction?" and "What do we do about it when we find one?" The answers are straightforward. We have source A, which appears to contradict source B. Let us imagine that source B does not exist. What does source A tell us after careful study? Then let us imagine that source A does not exist. What does source B tell us after careful study? Does source A alone completely agree with source B alone? If it does not agree completely, how completely does it agree? Using this test we find that there are indeed contradictions in the Bible. Now, what do we do with these contradictions? First we note that even if we throw out all the contradictory statements, we are still left with the vast majority of the Christian beliefs; and we are definitely left with all the central doctrines. Then we take contradictions one by one. For example, after the resurrection of Jesus, each of the authors gives a different person seeing Jesus first. If we only had one source, we would probably state with confidence who saw Jesus first. But because we have multiple accounts, we might assume that information has been lost. If we take it at face value, there is a clear contradiction. However, it is likely that Jesus met all the people in question, but each author recorded those visitations and ordered events to highlight the author's intended message. Another contradiction is how in the synoptics, Jesus almost never says "Amen, Amen I say to you," with two amens while he almost always does in John. In current writing exact quotes are the norm. However, in ancient written and oral traditions, variations in quotations are allowed, even expected, based upon the truth that the writer wishes to reveal. In John, this phrase is a synonym with, "Pay attention, what follows is important." This phrase gives the reader an outline of key points. Another example of a contradiction is the question of who bought The Field of Blood. Acts 1:18-20 indicates that it was Judas, while Mt 27:6-10 indicates that it was the chief priests. Any removal of this contradiction requires a rather strong stretching of what is written, which implies that at least one of the passages is historically inaccurate. However, who handed the money to the landowner and under exactly what circumstances is less important than the message of each evangelist, both of whom sought to show Judas's death as the fulfillment of scripture.

We must realize, though, that the existence of contradictions does mean that we must be careful not to take a single section out of context and hold it up as the final word on the matter. For now, we should read the Bible as the words of honest men who were reasonably close in time and distance to the actions and words of Jesus. These men are capable of making mistakes about non-vital details, and it is conceivable that they could make a mistake about an important detail or two. In order to believe, beyond a reasonable doubt, that something in the New Testament is true, we must see a pattern of verses with minimal contradiction. At it turns out, this is the case for every vital

Christian doctrine. Of course, I must demonstrate these one by one. This will be the approach for this book. However, note that after we see with eyes of faith (§ 6.1.7), a more God-centered understanding of scripture is more appropriate.

CHAPTER 5: Understanding Christianity, Using Scripture

5.1 God the Son

We have now arrived to the heart of the book. Based on the previous chapter, we will take scripture to be authoritative and use it to understand the core Christine doctrines, starting with the nature of Jesus. Figure 2 shows a map to guide us in the discussion. This will help us keep the dependencies of the arguments straight, as with our philosophical discussion (§ 3).

5.1.1 Believed in Elohim

Elohim is the Hebrew word for God, and is used frequently in the Old Testament.[17] Jesus was a Jew, and when Jesus speaks of God in the New Testament, it is clear that he means Elohim, the God of the Jews. He is usually speaking to Jews, and when

---

17   Elohim is actually the plural form of Eloah, which means that Elohim literally means gods rather than God. In the Hebrew Scriptures, it is necessary to use context to determine whether God or gods is meant. In addition, the plural Elohim can be understood to prefigure the New Testament understanding of the Trinity.

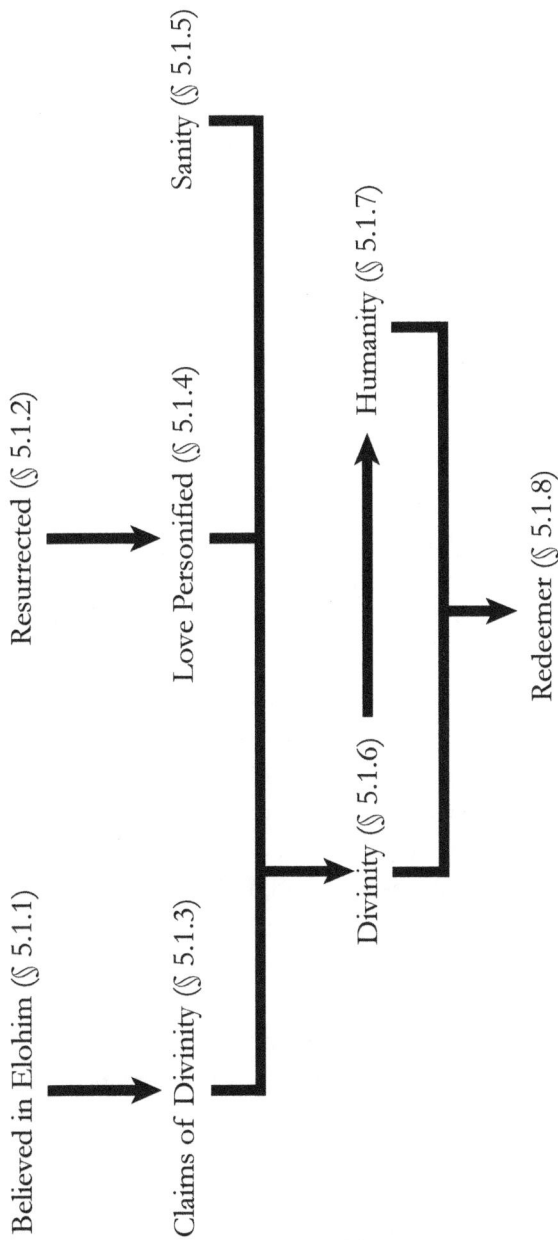

Figure 2 Scriptural Defense of Our Understanding of Jesus

Believed in Elohim (§ 5.1.1)

Resurrected (§ 5.1.2)

Claims of Divinity (§ 5.1.3)

Love Personified (§ 5.1.4)

Sanity (§ 5.1.5)

Divinity (§ 5.1.6)

Humanity (§ 5.1.7)

Redeemer (§ 5.1.8)

he refers to God, there is no confusion about who he is talking about. He refers to Elohim in this example:

> "And concerning the resurrection of the dead, have you not read what was said to you by God, 'I am the God of Abraham, the God of Isaac, and the God of Jacob?' He is not the God of the dead but of the living." (Mt 22:31-32, from Ex 3:6)

Abraham, Isaac, and Jacob are known as the Jewish patriarchs, whose stories are told in Genesis. I will use the term Elohim to indicate God as Jews understand God.

5.1.2 Resurrected

As I've discussed (§ 4.2.3), we know when the New Testament authors are reliable:

The Event or Concept Must Be Important.

Uniquely among religions, Christianity directs us to look at one specific event. If Jesus was resurrected, then Christianity is probably true. We would certainly be required to study it in detail before deciding that it is wrong. If Jesus was not resurrected, Christianity is certainly false. You would be better off being a Muslim or a Jew, or perhaps something else. Some would say that Jesus has great value as a moral teacher, regardless of whether or not he was resurrected. This is simply false. If the apostles lied about the resurrection, then nothing in the New Testament can be trusted or be considered a useful moral guide. Without the resurrection, Christianity collapses.

There Must Be General Agreement among the Authors.

Every author agrees about the truth of the resurrection. Every Gospel story leads up to it, with it as its conclusion. The letter writers speak of it frequently.

Therefore, Jesus was resurrected.

Objection 1:

You may say, "Hey..... Wait a minute....." In fact, I would expect most non-Christians to say this. The reason is simple. You are not able to accept the possibility of miracles. Reread the discussion of miracles (§ 2.4) for my response.

Objection 2:

In my section on the reliability of the New Testament authors, I defend the statement that they would not make a mistake about an important event like this. However, because of its prevalence, I should specifically discuss the swoon theory. This theory states that Jesus didn't die, but went into a coma or something like it. He was then buried. Once he recovered, he showed himself to the disciples. They proceeded to horribly misinterpret the situation. There are two problems with this. The first is that Jesus would not stand for it. His disciples would be lying in his name. Read the Gospels, and you will see how Jesus would not be willing to do this. The second problem is that crucifixion is not something that you can just recover from in three days. If Jesus survived, he would be a crippled wreck of a man, which is not the sort of figure that would inspire the awe and devotion of his followers.

I also should mention the hallucination theory. In this one, the five hundred or more people who saw him after his death were hallucinating. This contradicts everything that we know about hallucinations. They do not occur to large groups of people. This "hallucination" hung around for forty days, held conversations, ate, the whole shebang. A person who believes this theory has to invent a miracle in order to disprove a miracle. It does not gain them anything, and is not really plausible enough to warrant much discussion.

5.1.3 Claims of Divinity

Now, let us look as Jesus's claims of divinity using the same method.

The Event or Concept Must Be Important.

Jesus's claims for himself are critically important. This is especially true if he claimed to be divine. If Jesus claimed to be divine, the New Testament authors would not sweep it under the rug because it would critically alter the person that they are representing. If Jesus did not claim divinity, the honest authors would not and could not invent this claim by embellishing their sources. Even if they were only somewhat honest they could not create this lie. To understand this, we must understand Jewish theology. All of the New Testament quotes the Old Testament (The Hebrew Bible) as authoritative; so we know that the New Testament authors, some of whom were Jews, took Jewish theology very seriously. To Jews, Elohim is the only entity worthy of worship as divine. This is doctrine of the strongest order. This is what makes Jews, Jews. Once a Jew accepts some other person or entity as divine, they cease to be a Jew. This understanding of Jewish theology is clearly visible in both the Old and New Testaments. From the Old Testament, we have the first commandment: "You shall have no other Gods but me" (Ex 20:1-6). We also have "Hear, O Israel! The LORD is our God, the LORD alone!" (Deut 6:4). From the New Testament, we see that Jesus's claims of divinity are what caused the Jewish leaders to push for his execution. His blasphemy was of the highest order. I will get to the quotes in a moment.

There Must Be General Agreement among The Authors.

Here, I will initially break the authors into three groups. There are the synoptics: Matthew, Mark, and Luke; there is John's Gospel; and there are the various letters. At first, the synoptic authors appear to be giving very different representations of what Jesus said about himself than John in his Gospel. It is commonly asserted that the Johannean writings make Jesus divine, while the synoptics do not. This is not the case. With honest analysis, we realize that the synoptics and John's Gospel have the same understanding of Jesus. The only real difference is one of style. The synoptics state Jesus's divinity simply and only occasionally. The Gospel of John describes his divinity strongly and frequently. If the Gospel of John never existed, our understanding of Jesus would be much the same, though perhaps more muddled. In order to demonstrate this, I will emphasize what Jesus said in the synoptics and show the similarities in John. Paul and the other letter writers agree with the synoptic authors and John about what Jesus was, but they do not say as much about what Jesus actually said. What Paul and the other letter writers said about Jesus is important; but I will not discuss it much here, because here I am concerned primarily with what Jesus said about himself

Note that in future sections, I will not follow the above process so carefully, because the issues are less vital and less surprising after we already accept that Jesus was resurrected and claimed to be divine. However, if there is any particular point that you believe requires more care, I leave that to you as an exercise.

Messiah and The Son of God (Elohim)

All the Gospel writers are explicit that Jesus presented himself as the Messiah (the king of Israel promised in the Old Testament by God) and the Son of God. The synoptics all have the trial of Jesus before the Sanhedrin, a high Jewish court.

> "If you are the Messiah, tell us," but he [Jesus] replied to them, "If I tell you, you will not believe, and if I question, you will not respond. But from this time on the Son of Man will be seated at the right hand of the power of God." They all asked, "Are you

then the Son of God?" He replied to them, "You say that I am."
Then they said, "What further need have we for testimony? We
have heard it from his own mouth." (Lk 22:67-71; parallels in Mt
26:62-65; Mk 14:61-63)

The phrase, "You say that I am," is unclear in current usage,
but from the response of the council we have no doubt as to
its meaning. It means "You are correct." Notice that they say *the*
Son of God, not *a* Son of God. The Gospels are uniform on
this point. His blasphemy is to claim to be equal to God, as the
true Son of God must be. This is why the council immediately
wants to kill him.

John does not say explicitly what happens at the trial, but
he does imply that it occurred. See John, chapter 18. However,
Jesus does make the divinity and kingship claim explicitly
elsewhere in John. In Jn 1:49, he is called the Messiah and the
Son of God by Nathaniel. In Jn 20:28, he is called "My Lord
and my God!" by Thomas. Jesus confirms this identification
in both cases by accepting it without argument. In Jn 5:17-18,
some Jews attempt to kill Jesus because he states that he is the
Son of God.

These are not the only examples of when Jesus either refers
to himself as the Son of God and the Messiah or accepts that
acknowledgement.

> He said to them, "But who do you say that I am?" Simon Peter
> said in reply, "You are the Messiah, the Son of the living God."
> Jesus said to him in reply, "Blessed are you, Simon son of Jonah.
> For flesh and blood has not revealed this to you, but my heavenly
> Father." (Mt 16:15-17)

Jesus consistently refers to God as *his* Father, not *our* Father. See
Mt 18:10,19,35, 20:23, 21:33-41, 26:53; Lk 2:49; Mk 14:36; 120
places in John. The quote from Mark is especially telling. Here
he refers to God the Father as Abba, which translates to Dad
or Papa rather than Father. This implies an intimate relationship
with God that only a *true* son could have. The use of Father for

God is rare in the Jewish literature of the time and the use of Abba is non-existent.[18]

We see now that Jesus claimed explicitly to be *the* Son of God as well as the Messiah. Either this claim is true, or no man in history deserved to be crucified more than he.

Power to Forgive Sins

Jesus claims the power to forgive sins, and he supports this with miracles.

> They came bringing to him a paralytic carried by four men. Unable to get near Jesus because of the crowd, they opened up the roof above him. After they had broken through, they let down the mat on which the paralytic was lying. When Jesus saw their faith, he said to the paralytic, "Child, your sins are forgiven." Now some of the scribes were sitting there asking themselves, "Why does this man speak that way? He is blaspheming. Who but God alone can forgive sins?" Jesus immediately knew in his mind what they were thinking to themselves, so he said, "Why are you thinking such things in your hearts? Which is easier, to say to the paralytic, 'Your sins are forgiven,' or to say, 'Rise, pick up your mat and walk'? But that you may know that the Son of Man has authority to forgive sins on earth"– he said to the paralytic, "I say to you, rise, pick up you mat, and go home." He rose, picked up his mat at once, and went away in the sight of everyone. They were all astounded and glorified God, saying, "We have never seen anything like this." (Mk 2:3-12; parallels in Mt 9:2-7; Lk 5:18-26)

This story is not in John. In John, though, John the Baptist says that Jesus takes away the sins of the world; and Jesus accepts this honor (Jn 1:29). Now you may ask, "Why is forgiveness of sins a sign of divinity?" C.S. Lewis said it best:

> Now unless the speaker is God, this is really so preposterous as to be comic. We can all understand how a man forgives offences against himself. You tread on my toe and I forgive you, you steal my money and I forgive you. But what should we make of a man,

---

18   Joachim Jeremias, *New Testament Theology*, p. 66.

himself unrobbed and untrodden on, who announced that he forgave you for treading on other men's toes and stealing other men's money? Asinine fatuity is the kindest description we should give of his conduct. Yet this is what Jesus did. He told people that their sins were forgiven, and never waited to consult all the other people whom their sins had undoubtedly injured. He unhesitatingly behaved as if He was the party chiefly concerned, the person chiefly offended in all offences. This makes sense only if He really was the God whose laws are broken and whose love is wounded in every sin. In the mouth of any speaker who is not God these words would imply what I can only regard as a silliness unrivalled by any other character in history. (*Mere Christianity*, Book 2, Chapter 3)

Full Equality with Elohim

Jesus also made many explicit claims that he was equal to Elohim. Most of these claims are in John and Matthew, but we have already seen so much evidence in Mark and Luke that these claims are to a large degree superfluous. I include them for completeness and to bury you in the evidence.

> Then Jesus approached and said to them, "All power in heaven and on earth has been given to me. Go, therefore, and make disciples of all nations, baptizing them in the name of the Father, and of the Son, and of the holy Spirit, teaching them to observe all that I have commanded you. And behold, I am with you always, until the end of the age." (Mt 28:18-20)

> "I [Jesus] pray for them. I do not pray for the world but for the ones you [Elohim] have given me, because they are yours, and everything of mine is yours and everything of yours is mine, and I have been glorified in them." (Jn 17:9-10)

> "All things have been handed over to me by my Father. No one knows the Son except the Father, and no one knows the Father except the Son and anyone to whom the Son wishes to reveal him." (Mt 11:27)

> "No one can come to me unless the Father who sent me draw him, and I will raise him on the last day. It is written in the prophets:
> 'They shall all be taught by God.'

Everyone who listens to my Father and learns from him comes to me. Not that anyone has seen the Father except the one who is from God; he has seen the Father." (Jn 6:44-46)

The father and Jesus are in each other – they are one. (see Jn 10:30-39)

Jesus said we could do nothing of significance without having a right relationship with him. (see Jn 15:1-8)

Jesus spoke of the future church as *his* church and that they would meet in *his* name. (see Mt 16:18, 18:20)

To know him was to know God (Jn 8:19, 14:7); to see him was to see God (Jn 12:45, 14:9); to believe in him was to believe in God (Jn 12:44); to receive him was to receive God (Mk 9:37); to hate him was to hate God (Jn 15:23); and to honor him was to honor God (Jn 5:23).

Conclusion

We now can be sure, beyond a reasonable doubt, that Jesus said that he was *the* Son of God the Father, with all the rights, privileges, and duties thereof. This is a necessary, but not sufficient, condition to know that Jesus *is* the Son of God.

5.1.4 Love Personified

We know that Jesus was resurrected. Before he was resurrected, he was crucified. There is no way to get to the resurrection without the crucifixion. Now the pain of crucifixion is difficult to imagine. For most people, the worst experience of our lives does not really compare to the agony of being crucified. We know that Jesus knew that he was going to be crucified. See Mt 16:21-22, 17:22-23, 20:17-19; Mk 8:31-33, 9:30-32, 10:32-34; Lk 9:22, 9:43-45, 18:31-34; Jn 12:23-25, 32-33. Then why did he enter Jerusalem? Why did he not run in the other direction? Any place in the world would have been safer for him. He then goes around Jerusalem picking fights with the elders who would then push for his execution. He was not wrong to expose the hypocrisy of the elders, but he was not really required to do so either. The only reasonable conclusion is that he fully accepted his crucifixion. Even though the agony of crucifixion is extreme, there was some greater good that would be served by his death. What good is this? The first good of the crucifixion is the forgiveness of our sins, which deserves its own section (§ 5.1.8). The second good is the resurrection. What good is the resurrection, really? The resurrection is a lightning bolt in the heart of each of us that causes us to stand up and take notice of the words and actions of Jesus. At the center of what Jesus stood for is the Greatest Commandments:

> When the Pharisees heard that he had silenced the Sadducees, they gathered together, and one of them [a scholar of the law] tested him by asking, "Teacher, which commandment in the law is the greatest?" He said to them, "You shall love the Lord, your God, with all your heart, with all your soul, and with all your mind. This is the greatest and the first commandment. The second is like it: You shall love your neighbor as yourself. The whole law and the prophets depend on these two commandments." (Mt 22:34-40; parallels in Mk 12:28-34; Lk 10:25-28; from Old Testament Dt 6:5, Lv 19:18)

In case you are worried that the second commandment is a bit weak, realize that Jesus strengthened it:

> "This is my commandment: love one another as I love you. No one has greater love than this, to lay down one's life for one's friends." (Jn 15:12-13)

Jesus's actions are a total fulfillment of these commandments. In the end, he had two choices. One was to leave town and lead a normal life. The other was to be killed in one of the more horrible ways that man has devised. The first option is the option of selfishness, which would be easy to take. The other option is the option of love – true, complete, and self-giving love. This requires love like the world only rarely experiences.

This is the love that Jesus personified. It is not enough to say that Jesus loved. It is more accurate to say that Jesus was Love. As we will come to see, it is more accurate still to say that Jesus *is* Love, but I have not yet shown that Jesus is present today. His love is such that he gave himself so that our sins may be forgiven, so that we may follow and love God the Father, and so that we may love each other.

Some Side Notes

If you are reading my arguments carefully, you will have noticed that I have not yet demonstrated (using scripture) that a God exists that should be loved; but I used Jesus's love of the Father in my arguments. I am not assuming what I am trying to show, because if for some reason Jesus loved something that does not exist, it does not change the fact that he loved. Of course, if Jesus died for something that did not exist, it would be a sad travesty; but I have not yet shown that Christianity is not a sad travesty. I'll be getting to that shortly.

By only focusing on one event, I may have given you the false impression that this is all that we know about the love of Jesus. This is not the case. Throughout the Gospels, the message of Jesus never gets far from the message of love. Rather than me going through examples, however, it is much better if you read the Gospels and experience them for yourself.

5.1.5 Sanity

I will now demonstrate that Jesus was sane. You may ask: why do I need to do this? I have shown that he believed that he was equal with God. One possible explanation for this is that he was not all together upstairs. I must debunk this possibility. First I must ask, what does it mean to be insane? Insanity is having a dramatically false perception of reality. Perception of reality can be divided into the categories of perception of self, others, the natural, and the supernatural. When a person is not sane in one category, this insanity leaks into the other categories to a greater or lesser degree. Conversely, the more sane a person is, the more accurate their understanding of reality is in each of these categories. Usually, we measure the sanity of a person on the basis of their grasp of the first three categories; but sometimes we can see dramatic problems in the fourth category. I am not saying that the last category is less important. It is just more difficult to say if someone is insane based his or her understanding of the supernatural because it is difficult to get a strong grasp of the supernatural. Using my definition of sane, a perfectly sane person will have a correct understanding of the supernatural as well as the other categories, and very few people are perfectly sane. Most people are sane enough to get by, however.

Now, how do we decide if Jesus was sane? We must look at the Bible, while trusting the New Testament authors; and ask how well he perceived reality. We can't ask if he was sane on the basis of his perception of himself because we want to use his sanity to help show that his perception of himself was correct. The Bible is very thin on Jesus's understanding of the natural world, so we cannot use that. We cannot use Jesus's understanding of the supernatural as a test for sanity because even though Jesus is very explicit about it, honest men disagree about the true reality of the supernatural. Fortunately, the Bible has much information about Jesus's understanding of others. His understanding of human nature in general and in particular is exquisite. It is not possible to believe that such a strong understanding of others and a deranged view of self could exist in the same person. I will go through two examples to demonstrate his understanding of human nature.

Jesus showed his clarity of understanding most clearly when he was challenged. The longest recorded debate between Jesus and the Jewish elders is in Matthew, chapter 22, with parallels in Mark, chapter 12 and Luke, chapter 20. In these debates he is able to easily dispatch all intellectual challenges. He can only do this because of his extremely strong understanding of the Jewish elders, the Jewish law, and human nature. To pull out one example from this debate:

> Then the Pharisees went off and plotted how they might entrap him in speech. They sent their disciples to him, with the Herodians, saying, "Teacher, we know that you are a truthful man and that you teach the way of God in accordance with the truth. And you are not concerned with anyone's opinion, for you do not regard a person's status. Tell us, then, what is your opinion: Is it lawful to pay the census tax to Caesar or not?" Knowing their malice, Jesus said, "Why are you testing me, you hypocrites? Show me the coin that pays the census tax." Then they handed him the Roman coin. He said to them, "Whose image is this and whose inscription?" They replied, "Caesar's." At that he said to them, "Then repay to Caesar what belongs to Caesar and to God what belongs to God." When they heard this they were amazed, and leaving him they went away. (Mt 22:15-22; parallels in Mk 12:13-17; and Lk 20:20-26)

If you are not familiar with this story, you may not understand how this question was a trap. If Jesus said, "You must not pay the census tax," he would anger the Roman authorities and be branded as a revolutionary. If he said, "You must pay the census tax," he would anger the Jewish authorities because the coin said that Caesar was divine. He would be labeled as a traitor to Judaism. Not only was he able to evade the trap, but he was able to shock them back into realizing what is truly important. If he was insane, he would not have this clarity of understanding. He understood that the discussion should not be about the Jews verses the Romans, but about that which belongs to God and that which does not. In the legalistic mindset of the Jews of the day, they had forgotten that God is what is important, not taxation practices.

Now, I will pull an example from the Gospel of John:

> Then the scribes and the Pharisees brought a woman who had been caught in adultery and made her stand in the middle. They said to him, "Teacher, this woman was caught in the very act of

committing adultery. Now in the law, Moses commanded us to stone such women. So what do you say?" They said this to test him, so that they could have some charge to bring against him. Jesus bent down and began to write on the ground with his finger. But when they continued asking him, he straightened up and said to them, "Let the one among you who is without sin be the first to throw a stone at her." Again he bent down and wrote on the ground. And in response, they went away one by one, beginning with the elders. So he was left alone with the woman before him. Then Jesus straightened up and said to her, "Woman, where are they? Has no one condemned you?" She replied, "No one, sir." Then Jesus said, "Neither do I condemn you. Go, and from now on do not sin any more." (Jn 8:3-11)

Here, the trap is that if Jesus said to stone her, he is not following his message of love and forgiveness. If he says to not stone her, then he is breaking the law of Moses. Again, he takes a third path by true understanding of his challengers. He knows that none of them is without sin, so none of them can kill the adulterous woman without being a hypocrite. He uses this to shame them into forgiving the woman. Again, it is inconceivable that this sort of clarity can come from a person who has a weak grip on reality.

These two examples deal with Jesus's understanding of human nature in specific cases. Both of these cases demonstrate Jesus's ability to pierce the pretenses of people and pull them back to what is important. This was one of Jesus's strongest talents, and it is readily in evidence throughout the New Testament. Therefore, we know that he was sane. This is a necessary, but not sufficient, condition to know that Jesus is divine.

5.1.6 Divinity[19]

We know that Jesus claimed to be divine. There are only three possible reasons for this. He is a liar, he is insane, or he is correct. There is no other option. We know that Jesus personified love. It is not conceivable that a false claim of divinity would be the path that a loving person would take. Therefore, Jesus was not lying. We have shown that Jesus was sane. Therefore, there is no other possibility but to accept Jesus's claims at face value. That is, Jesus was divine and equal to Elohim. Because Jesus is divine and honest, once we have shown that he believes something to be true, we have shown it to be true. Ordinarily, I do not use arguments by authority, but we have shown that Jesus is no ordinary authority.

To get a first pass understanding of Jesus's divinity, reread his claims about himself, but now understand them to be true. To get a deeper understanding, learn about God the Father (§ 5.2); and then realize that Jesus is in no way less than God the Father, only different. Paul often describes this as Jesus sitting at the right hand of the Father (Rom 8:34; Eph 1:20; Col 3:1; for example), and is referencing Ps 110:1. Jesus's all-loving nature is apparent. However, what about the Father's omnipotence and omniscience? Why did Jesus not heal all people if he had the power? The question is a direct reference to the problem of pain (§ 2.1). As discussed in that section, there is no requirement that God remove all pain just because he can. Because Jesus is God, he has the same lack of restriction. The greater good is served by Jesus not healing all people.

We should also mention God's relationship with time and space (§ 3.6). God is outside space-time and not bound by it. Every divine person must exist at all times. Therefore, we have

---

19   The arguments in this and in the immediately preceding sections borrow a fair amount from C.S. Lewis, *Mere Christianity*, Chapter 3, and Kreeft and Tacelli, *Handbook of Christian Apologetics*, Chapter 7.

the teaching of the pre-incarnate Son of God. Because the Father and the Son have always existed, the relation between them, the birthing if you will, is eternal as well. The Father did not make the Son. The Son is begotten by the Father, God from God, Light from Light, true God from true God. For scriptural confirmation of this teaching, see Mk 12:36-37; Jn 1:1-15, 6:62, 8:58, 12:41, 17:5, 24-25.

Because the Son has existed since the beginning and is a full equal with the Father, he must also have a hand in creation. It is not clear from what we have learned already exactly what this relationship to creation must be. However, we learn from the Bible that through Jesus, all things were made (Jn 1:1-15; Col 1:16; Heb 1:2). What this means is that Jesus acts as the interface between the Father and creation. We will learn shortly that Jesus is also the interface between the Father and humanity.

Before going too much farther, it is important to realize that Jesus is fully human, as well as being fully divine.

5.1.7 Humanity

We must realize that Jesus is not God in a man suit. This belief is not common these days; but it has existed in much of Church history and would be an understandable mistake for a new Christian to make. Jesus is really and truly human as well as being really and truly divine. When reading the Gospels, it is apparent that Jesus has all the characteristics of being a man. He is born, suffers, and dies. He assures the disciples of the reality of his body (Lk 24:38-43). He exists finitely in time and space. Paul speaks of Jesus as a man (Rom 5:15; 1 Cor 15:21; 1 Tim 2:5) and speaks of his human origin (Rom 1:3, 9:5; 2 Tim 2:8; Gal 3:16, 4:4). Not only does Jesus have a human body, but he has a human soul, as Jesus himself tells us (Mt 26:38; Lk 23:46). Finally, Jesus frequently refers to himself as being the Son of Man (Mt 16:27; Mk 2:28; Lk 5:24; Jn 5:27; and many others), which indicates that he sees himself as human.

How is it possible to be both human and divine? Even though our instincts say that this must be contradictory, upon further inspection no contradiction is apparent. We see Jesus acting both as man and God throughout the Gospels. We must trust the data before we trust our own biases about the way things are "supposed" to be.

When did his humanity begin? To be human means to be limited in time and to be born of flesh, so his humanity must have begun at the moment of conception, which makes Mary his true mother, not just a temporary residence. This is confirmed by scripture (Mt 1:16; Lk 1:31; Gal 4:4). How does his humanity begin? It begins by the power of the Holy Spirit. This is explicitly stated in scripture (Mt 1:18-21; Lk 1:34-35) and can also be further understood because the Holy Spirit is the giver of life (§ 5.3.3). All three members of the Trinity are involved in the incarnation: Father, Son, and Spirit. When does his humanity end? It does not, as our humanity does not. In addition, scripture teaches that after he was resurrected, he spent some time with the disciples, and then he ascended into Heaven (Mk 16:19; Lk 24:50-51; Jn 1:51), and that he will be with us always (Mt 28:20). He ascended intact. His body and soul were not left behind or destroyed in the process. At first, ascension seems strange, but after the resurrection any other departure for Jesus would be stranger. It would be awfully silly to be resurrected and just die again a short while later. If he had lived to old age, we would certainly have a record of it. There is also evidence from scripture that Jesus's resurrected body is fundamentally different as he is not easily recognized by his followers (Lk 24:15-16). Because we know that he beat death once, it is unclear that he could have died after he was resurrected.

The humanity of Jesus teaches us that God understands us directly, not purely intellectually. Additionally, if Jesus was God in a man suit, the suffering of Jesus would be meaningless, because Jesus must be a man to suffer. This leads us to our next topic, Jesus as redeemer.

5.1.8 Redeemer

Before discussing redemption, it is necessary to discuss sin. First, realize that sin is defined as "An injury or break in a person's relationship with God." Today, sin (especially private sin) is scoffed at in much of Western culture. This follows directly from the way that God is scoffed at in much of Western culture. To acknowledge a God who loves us is to acknowledge our ability to injure our relationship with God. Jesus is very explicit about the reality of sin and our need to repair our relationship with God. Once we honestly accept Christianity, it becomes readily apparent that our relationship with God is broken. We typically go through a phase of trying to fix ourselves without assistance from anyone. We soon find that this is inadequate. We must reach out for the assistance of Jesus, which is given to all who ask for it.

Jesus is our redeemer in several ways. First, we have spoken previously of Jesus's forgiveness of sins (§ 5.1.3). To ask Jesus's forgiveness is to receive it. Thus, Jesus washes away past sin. Forgiveness of sins is so important to Jesus that he instituted two formal mechanisms by which sin could be washed away: Baptism and Reconciliation. In Baptism (Mt 28:19), we are initiated into the Church. This necessitates that our past transgressions will not be held against us, so our sins must be forgiven. We are born again (Jn 3:1-8) into Jesus (Rom 6:3). Our old lives are washed away (1 Pet 3:21) and replaced with new lives in God. However, we do not always live up to the expectations of our new life. For this, Jesus instituted Reconciliation (Mt 16:19, 18:18; Jn 20:21-23). Only God can forgive sins (§ 5.1.3). However, Jesus shared that power with specific men, whom we now call priests. Since Jesus is no longer with us in the flesh, he provided a necessary human element to assist in our Reconciliation to him. The priest is an intermediary for Jesus, who acts in and through the priest to offer us forgiveness.

Second, Jesus is a guide. Jesus is the redeemer, not only by forgiving past sins, but by leading us to a new life of love and holiness. He shows us how to live both by his acts and his teachings (§ 5.1.4).

Third, Jesus, in a very real way, takes the penalty for our sin. Without the pain of the crucifixion, there could not have been the glory of the resurrection. Without the glory of the resurrection, we would have no reason to accept the divinity of Jesus or his ability to forgive us. When Jesus instituted the Eucharist, he spoke of his sacrifice for our redemption:

> While they were eating, Jesus took bread, said the blessing, broke it, and giving it to his disciples said, "Take and eat; this is my body." Then he took a cup gave thanks, and gave it to them, saying, "Drink from it, all of you, for this is my blood of the covenant, which will be shed on behalf of many for the forgiveness of sins." (Mt 26:26-28; parallels in Mk 14:22-24; Lk 22:19-20)

He takes the punishment, and we get the reward. For additional scriptural defense, we have Is 53:7-12; Jn 1:29; Eph 5:2; 1 Cor 5:7; Rom 3:25; Hebr 9:1-28; 1 Jn 2:2. From these verses, we get a title of Jesus as the sacrificial Lamb of God.

Fourth, Jesus acts as the interface between us and God the Father; as he tells us, "I am the way, and the truth and the life. No one comes to the Father except through me" (Jn 14:6). If we only understand God using philosophy (§ 3), it can be difficult to have a deep personal relationship with God. This God is so great and ephemeral that it is difficult to understand how God could connect with us. Jesus, however, is both fully human (§ 5.1.7) and fully divine (§ 5.1.6). He provides a direct way for us humans to connect with God because he himself has that connection within him. In this way, Jesus redeems our humanity and connects us to divinity.

The central reason Jesus became man is in order to redeem us. He came to save us from our sin and to lead us to life with God. Jesus says, "For the Son of Man [Jesus] has come to seek and to save what was lost" (Lk 19:10), and "Go and learn the meaning of the words, 'I desire mercy, not sacrifice.' I did not come to call the righteous but sinners" (Mt 9:13). This teaching is also given by Isaiah (Is 35:4), elsewhere in the Gospels (Lk 2:11, 2:30; Jn 3:17) and in Paul's letters (1 Tim 1:15). Thus, we call Jesus Savior. Note that Jesus means God Saves (Mt 1:21).

In addition to being the redeemer, Jesus is also the judge. They must go together, because who, but the judge, can forgive the debts of anyone? In addition, we have the words of Jesus, "Nor does the Father judge anyone, but he has given all judgment to his Son, so that all may honor the Son just as they honor the Father" (Jn 5:22-23), and "When the Son of Man comes in his glory, and all the angels with him, he will sit upon his glorious throne, and all the nations will be assembled before him. And he will separate them one from another, as a shepherd separates the sheep from the goats" (Mt 25:31-32). To each person Jesus holds out his hand, and waits for us to take it. For those who do, the reward is glorious, for those of us who do not, the penalty is severe. Jesus gives various descriptions of the difference between Heaven and Hell. I quote one here:

> He proposed another parable to them. "The kingdom of heaven may be likened to a man who sowed good seed in his field. While everyone was asleep his enemy came and sowed weeds all through the wheat, and then went off. When the crop grew and bore fruit, the weeds appeared as well. The slaves of the householder came to him and said, 'Master, did you not sow good seed in your field? Where have the weeds come from?' He answered, 'An enemy has done this.' His slaves said to him, 'Do you want us to go and pull them up?' He replied, 'No, if you pull up the weeds you might uproot the wheat along with them. Let them grow together until harvest; then at harvest time I will say to the harvesters, "First collect the weeds and tie them in bundles for burning; but gather the wheat into my barn." ' " (Mt 13:24-30)

Jesus later explains:

> He said in reply, "He who sows good seed is the Son of Man, the field is the world, the good seed the children of the kingdom. The weeds are the children of the evil one, and the enemy who sows them is the devil. The harvest is the end of the age, and the harvesters are angels. Just as weeds are collected and burned with fire, so will it be at the end of the age. The Son of Man will send his angels, and they will collect out of his kingdom all who cause others to sin and all evildoers. They will throw them into the fiery furnace, where there will be wailing and grinding of teeth. Then the righteous will shine like the sun in the kingdom of their Father. Whoever has ears ought to hear." (Mt 13: 37-43)

To be the final judge, Jesus must also be the absolute lawgiver. Jesus asserts his lawgiving power (Jn 14:15, 15:10; Mt 28:20), and gives the law of love (Jn 13:34, 15:12), as well as many other commandments. Finally, note that to be the Judge and Lawgiver, Jesus must also be the King, because as Judge and Lawgiver he is the highest authority. In other words, in the celestial government, Jesus is all. Jesus asserts his kingship (Mk 8:29; Jn 4:25-26, 18:37; Mt 28:18), but that it is not of this world (Jn 6:15, 18:36). The name Christ is actually a title, meaning Anointed One, which is a translation of Messiah, the promised new King of Israel from the Old Testament (Ps 2, 45, 72; Is 9:1-6; Dn 7:13-15). Jews do not accept this understanding of Jesus, which corresponds with their rejection of the New Testament. Of course, any Jew who does accept the New Testament becomes a Christian; and is a Jew no longer.

At one level, the difference between glory and damnation is a legal one. Follow the specified laws; and you are good and rewarded; otherwise, you are bad and are punished. This is the understanding of Heaven and Hell that is typically parodied by non-Christians. Those that focus on this at the exclusion of other goals are missing the point. The laws are a crutch to prepare us for the goal, but they are not the goal. Others believe that getting into Heaven is like a driver's license exam. Have sufficient knowledge about and belief in Jesus, and you're in. Otherwise, you fail and are not allowed to enter. Knowledge of God helps lead us to the goal, but it is not the goal. To quote Paul:

> If I speak in human and angelic tongues but do not have love, I am a resounding gong or a clashing cymbal. And if I have the gift of prophecy and comprehend all mysteries and all knowledge; if I have all faith so as to move mountains but do not have love, I am nothing. If I give away everything I own, and if I hand my body over so that I may boast but do not have love, I gain nothing.
>
> Love is patient, love is kind. It is not jealous, [love] is not pompous, it is not inflated, it is not rude, it does not seek its own interests, it is not quick-tempered, it does not brood over injury, it does not rejoice over wrongdoing but rejoices with the truth. It bears all things, believes all things, hopes all things, endures all things.
>
> Love never fails. If there are prophecies, they will be brought to nothing; if tongues, they will cease; if knowledge, it will be brought to nothing. For we know partially and we prophesy partially, but when the perfect comes, the partial will pass away. When I was a child, I used to talk as a child, think as a child, reason as a child; when I became a man, I put aside childish things. At present we see indistinctly, as in a mirror, but then face to face. At present I know partially; then I show know fully, as I am fully known. So faith, hope, love remain, these three; but the greatest of these is love. (1 Cor 13)

The goal is acceptance of Love, or equivalently, the acceptance of God, because God is Love (1 Jn 4:8). We must realize that God loves everyone infinitely. What is different is how we respond to that love. After death, there is no avoiding God. To love God is to feel the ecstasy of true love consummated, completely and perfectly. To hate God is to be unable to escape. Wherever you go, God is there. Whatever you do, God is wrapping himself around, beside, and inside you. To be truly intimate with that which you hate is infinite torture. With this understanding, we realize that the fire of Hell is the love of God, rejected.

However, many of us are not completely ready for true intimacy with God. There is some sin that we are not ready to give up, but we do love God, so Hell is not appropriate either. For this reason, we understand that if you die in this state you will feel both Heaven and Hell imperfectly. In so far as you are in a state of love you feel the joy of Heaven. In so far as you are in a state of sin, you feel the pain of Hell. In the process, the fires of this domain, called Purgatory, burn away the sin, and leave only the joy. Scripture speaks of the possibility of the forgiveness of sins after death (2 Mac 12:46; Mt 5:26, 12:31-32) and that the process can be painful, as in fire (1 Cor 3:15; 1 Pet 1:7).

5.2 God the Father

Now we can move to a discussion of God the Father. First, know that when Jesus talks about God the Father, he is referring to Elohim, the God of the Jews (§ 5.1.1). I will now list a fairly complete summary of what Jesus taught about Elohim. Even though his emphasis is sometimes different, he does not contradict the teachings of the Old Testament. Because we know that we can trust Jesus (§ 5.1.6), the following are all true. If you compare the God revealed by Jesus with the God we deduced from philosophy (§ 3), you will see many similarities and no contradictions. However, the God of the Bible is much more personal and intimate than the God of philosophy as we shall see. If we look at the whole Bible, we can get a fuller picture of God; but I show below that the words of Jesus alone are enough to get all the key points.

5.2.1 Creator

All Jews know that God was the creator of all things, so Jesus did not need to expound on this at great length, but he does mention it in passing while discussing other topics. God is the first cause as described in Genesis. God is not merely the cause, but the creator, which implies a personal interaction with creation rather than a mechanical one.

> "But from the beginning of creation, 'God made them male and female.'" (Mk 10:6; Gn 1:27)

> "For those times will have tribulation such as has not been since the beginning of God's creation until now, nor ever will be." (Mk 13:19)

5.2.2 Omniscient

Jesus spoke frequently about the omniscient (all-knowing) nature of the Father. He knows not only all the details of what is happening in the universe, but also knows what is in our hearts.

> "But when you give alms, do not let your left hand know what your right is doing, so that your almsgiving may be secret. And your Father who sees in secret will repay you." (Mt 6:3-4)

> "Do not be like them. Your Father knows what you need before you ask him." (Mt 6:8)

> "But when you fast, anoint your head and wash your face, so that you may not appear to be fasting, except to your Father who is hidden. And your Father who sees what is hidden will repay you." (Mt 6:17-18)

> "Are not two sparrows sold for a small coin? Yet not one of them falls to the ground without your Father's knowledge. Even all the hairs of your head are counted." (Mt 10:29-30; parallel in Lk 12:7)

> "But of that day and hour no one knows, neither the angels of heaven, nor the Son, but the Father alone." (Mt 24:36; parallel in Mk 13:32)

And he said to them, "You justify yourselves in the sight of others, but God knows your hearts; for what is of human esteem is an abomination in the sight of God." (Lk 16:15)

5.2.3 Omnipotent

Not only is God all-knowing, but he is all-powerful as well.

Jesus looked at them and said, "For human beings this is impossible, but for God all things are possible." (Mt 19:26; parallels in Mk 10:27; Lk 18:27)

5.2.4 Glory Of

In addition, Jesus taught that the Father is worthy to be glorified.

"This is how you are to pray:
Our Father in heaven,
hallowed be your name." (Mt 6:9)

"Father, glorify your name." Then a voice came from heaven, "I have glorified it and will glorify it again." (Jn 12:28)

"And whatever you ask in my name, I will do, so that the Father may be glorified in the Son." (Jn 14:13)

5.2.5 Father

Next, we see that the term Father is not merely a metaphor. He is truly our Father, and loves as a good Father should. In turn, our proper relationship to him is that of children not subjects or slaves.

"If you then, who are wicked, know how to give good gifts to your children, how much more will your heavenly Father give good things to those who ask him." (Mt 7:11; parallels in Mk 11:24; Lk 11:9-13)

"But I say to you, love your enemies and pray for those who persecute you, that you may be children of your heavenly Father, for he makes his sun rise on the bad and the good, and causes rain to fall on the just and the unjust." (Mt 5:44-45; parallel in Lk 6:35)

5.2.6 All Loving

Regardless of our mistakes, imperfections, and willful disobedience, our divine Father is always there waiting and urging us to return to him.

"Therefore I tell you, do not worry about your life, what you will eat [or drink], or about your body, what you will wear. Is not life more than food and the body more than clothing? Look at the birds in the sky; they do not sow or reap, they gather nothing into barns, yet your heavenly Father feeds them. Are not you more important than they? Can any of you by worrying add a single moment to your life-span? Why are you anxious about clothes? Learn from the way the wild flowers grow. They do not work or spin. But I tell you that not even Solomon in all his splendor was clothed like one of them. If God so clothes the grass of the field, which grows today and is thrown into the oven tomorrow, will he not much more provide for you, O you of little faith? So do not worry and say, 'What are we to eat?' or 'What are we to drink?' or 'What are we to wear?' All these things the pagans seek. Your heavenly Father knows that you need them all. But seek first the kingdom [of God] and his righteousness, and all these things will be given you besides. Do not worry about tomorrow; tomorrow will take care of itself. Sufficient for a day is its own evil." (Mt 6:25-34)

It may be that you believe the teachings of Christianity, but believe that you cannot be a Christian for a different reason. The argument is the following:

"If God knows anything about me, and he knows everything about me, then he will not want to have anything to do with me. I've stolen, lied, slept with half the town, murdered, etcetera. Christians are holy, and I can never be holy. I have already been condemned, and nothing can change that."

As is often the case, Jesus has the best answer for this, which he tells in the form of parable of the lost sheep.

> "What man among you having a hundred sheep and losing one of them would not leave the ninety-nine in the desert and go after the lost one until he finds it? And when he does find it, he sets it on his shoulders with great joy and, upon his arrival home, he calls together his friends and neighbors and says to them, 'Rejoice with me because I have found my lost sheep.' I tell you in just the same way there will be more joy in heaven over one sinner who repents than over ninety-nine righteous people who have no need of repentance." (Lk 15:4-7; parallel in Mt 18:11-14)

There is also the parable of the prodigal son.

> Then he [Jesus] said, "A man had two sons, and the younger son said to his father, 'Father, give me the share of your estate that should come to me.' So the father divided the property between them. After a few days, the younger son collected all his belongings and set off to a distant country where he squandered his inheritance on a life of dissipation. When he had freely spent everything, a severe famine struck that country, and he found himself in dire need. So he hired himself out to one of the local citizens who sent him to his farm to tend the swine. And he longed to eat his fill of the pods on which the swine fed, but nobody gave him any. Coming to his senses he thought, 'How many of my father's hired workers have more than enough food to eat, but here am I, dying from hunger. I shall get up and go to my father and I shall say to him, "Father, I have sinned against heaven and against you. I no longer deserve to be called your son; treat me as you would treat one of your hired workers." ' So he got up and went back to his father. While he was still a long way off, his father caught sight of him, and was filled with compassion. He ran to his son, embraced him and kissed him. His son said to him, 'Father, I have sinned against heaven and against you; I no longer deserve to be called your son.' But his father ordered his servants, 'Quickly bring the finest robe and put it on him; put a ring on his finger and sandals on his feet. Take the fattened calf and slaughter it. Then let us celebrate with a feast, because this son of mine was dead, and has come to life again; he was lost, and has been found.' Then the celebration began." (Lk 15:11-24)

No matter who you are, or what you have done, God still loves you and wants you to come home because he is your Father. Unlike human parents, however, God is a perfect parent: "Can a mother forget her infant, be without tenderness for the child of her womb? Even should she forget, I will never forget you" (Is 49:15). Some Christians find it disturbing that those who have sinned are not sufficiently punished for their sins when they repent. Jesus has an answer for them, in the continuation of the parable of the prodigal son:

> "Now the older son had been out in the field and, on his way back, as he neared the house, he heard the sound of music and dancing. He called one of the servants and asked what this might mean. The servant said to him, 'Your brother has returned and your father has slaughtered the fattened calf because he has him back safe and sound.' He became angry, and when he refused to enter the house, his father came out and pleaded with him. He said to his father in reply, 'Look, all these years I served you and not once did I disobey your orders; yet you never gave me even a young goat to feast on with my friends. But when your son returns who swallowed up your property with prostitutes, for him you slaughter the fattened calf.' He said to him, 'My son, you are here with me always; everything I have is yours. But now we must celebrate and rejoice, because your brother was dead and has come to life again; he was lost and has been found.' " (Lk 15:25-32)

Finally, I must warn you that your repentance must be genuine. You cannot scam God and tell him that you have repented, but continue with your old life. It is vital that every time you fall, you must repent again and strive to do better. It may take many cycles of sin and repentance before you are truly home, but with every cycle, you will be closer.

5.2.7 Merciful

Because the Father loves us, it also follows that he is merciful to us when we repent.

There is the parable of the lost sheep, same as above. (see Lk 15:4-7)

There is the parable of the prodigal son, same as above. (see Lk 15:11-24)

"If you forgive others their transgressions, your heavenly Father will forgive you." (Mt 6:14)

"Be merciful, just as [also] your Father is merciful." (Lk 6:36)

"This is how you are to pray:
    Our Father in heaven,
    hallowed be your name,
    your kingdom come,
    your will be done,
        on earth as in heaven.
    Give us today our daily bread;
    and forgive us our debts,
        as we forgive our debtors;
    and do not subject us to the final test,
        but deliver us from the evil one."
(Mt 6:9-13; parallel in Lk 11:2)

"That is why the kingdom of heaven may be likened to a king who decided to settle accounts with his servants. When he began the accounting, a debtor was brought before him who owed him a huge amount. Since he had no way of paying it back, his master ordered him to be sold, along with his wife, his children, and all his property, in payment of the debt. At that, the servant fell down, did him homage, and said, 'Be patient with me, and I will pay you back in full.' Moved with compassion the master of that servant let him go and forgave him the loan." (Mt 18:23-27)

5.2.8 Just

Though he loves us, his love is not blind. If we are not ready for him, our sins will have consequences. If we – in the final analysis – reject him, then he will grant us our desire. That he loves us as persons rather than animals requires that he honor our will, no matter how bad it is for us.

> [continuation from above] "When that servant had left, he found one of his fellow servants who owed him a much smaller amount. He seized him and started to choke him, demanding, 'Pay back what you owe.' Falling to his knees, his fellow servant begged him, 'Be patient with me, and I will pay you back.' But he refused. Instead, he had him put in prison until he paid back the debt. Now when his fellow servants saw what had happened, they were deeply disturbed, and went to their master and reported the whole affair. His master summoned him and said to him, 'You wicked servant! I forgave you your entire debt because you begged me to. Should you not have had pity on your fellow servant, as I had pity on you?' Then in anger his master handed him over to the torturers until he should pay back the whole debt. So will my heavenly Father do to you, unless each of you forgives his brother from his heart." (Mt 18:28-35)

> "When you stand to pray, forgive anyone against whom you have a grievance, so that your heavenly Father may in turn forgive you your transgressions." (Mk 11:25)

> "The rest laid hold of his servants, mistreated them, and killed them. The king was enraged and sent his troops, destroyed those murderers, and burned their city." (Mt 22:6-7)

> "Then the king said to his attendants, 'Bind his hands and feet, and cast him into the darkness outside, where there will be wailing and grinding of teeth.' " (Mt 22:13)

5.3 God the Spirit

Most of our knowledge of the Holy Spirit comes from the experience of the apostles, recorded in the Acts of the Apostles. While the Gospels are primarily about our experience of God in the person of Jesus, the Acts are primarily about our experience of God the Spirit. Though most of our knowledge of the Spirit comes from Acts, Jesus does have some teachings about the Spirit.

5.3.1 Given Freely

There are two important points in this section. The first is that the Spirit is a gift, given freely. All that is necessary is for us to allow him in. The second point is that he is the gift of both God the Father and God the Son. Jesus promised that after his departure, he and God the Father would send the Holy Spirit to assist the apostles in their mission to spread the message of God. The Holy Spirit is also referred to as the Advocate or the Spirit of truth.

> On the last and greatest day of the feast, Jesus stood up and exclaimed, "Let anyone who thirsts come to me and drink. Whoever believes in me, as scripture says:
> 'Rivers of living water will flow from within him.'"
> He said this in reference to the Spirit that those who came to believe in him were to receive. There was, of course, no Spirit yet, because Jesus had not yet been glorified. (Jn 7:37-39)

> "And I will ask the Father, and he will give you another Advocate to be with you always, the Spirit of truth, which the world cannot accept, because it neither sees nor knows it. But you know it, because it remains with you, and will be in you." (Jn 14:16-17)

> "When the Advocate comes whom I will send you from the Father, the Spirit of truth that proceeds from the Father, he will testify to me. And you also testify, because you have been with me from the beginning." (Jn 15:26-27)

> And when he said this, he breathed on them and said to them, "Receive the holy Spirit." (Jn 20:22)

In John, the Holy Spirit is given to the apostles shortly after the resurrection. In Luke-Acts, the Holy Spirit was promised shortly after the resurrection, but is not actually given until fifty days after the resurrection, at the event that we call Pentecost.

Both writers agree, however, about what the Spirit is, and what he represents.

> You are witnesses of these things. And [behold] I am sending the promise of my Father upon you; but stay in the city until you are clothed with power from on high." (Lk 24:48-49)

> In the first book, Theophilus, I dealt with all that Jesus did and taught until the day he was taken up, after giving instructions through the holy Spirit to the apostles whom he had chosen. He presented himself alive to them by many proofs after he had suffered, appearing to them during forty days and speaking about the kingdom of God. While meeting with them, he enjoined them not to depart from Jerusalem, but to wait for "the promise of the Father about which you have heard me seek; for John baptized with water, but in a few days you will be baptized with the holy Spirit." ...

> "But you will receive power when the holy Spirit comes upon you, and you will be my witnesses in Jerusalem, throughout Judea and Samaria, and to the ends of the earth." (Acts 1:1-5,8)

> When the time for Pentecost was fulfilled, they were all in one place together. And suddenly there came from the sky a noise like a strong driving wind, and it filled the entire house in which they were. Then there appeared to them tongues as of fire, which parted and came to rest on each one of them. And they were all filled with the holy Spirit and began to speak in different tongues, as the Spirit enabled them to proclaim.

> Now there were devout Jews from every nation under heaven staying in Jerusalem. At this sound, they gathered in a large crowd, but they were confused because each one heard them speaking in his own language. They were astounded, and in amazement they asked, "Are not all these people who are speaking Galileans? Then how does each of us hear them in his own native language?" (Acts 2:1-8)

The gift of the Holy Spirit did not end with the apostles. God continues to give out the Holy Spirit as the church grows in Acts.

While Peter was still speaking these things, the holy Spirit fell upon all who were listening to the word. The circumcised believers who had accompanied Peter were astounded that the gift of the holy Spirit should have been poured out on the Gentiles also, for they could hear them speaking in tongues and glorifying God. Then Peter responded, "Can anyone withhold the water for baptizing these people, who have received the holy Spirit even as we have?" (Acts 10:44-47)

While Apollos was in Corinth, Paul traveled through the interior of the country and came to Ephesus where he found some disciples. He said to them, "Did you receive the holy Spirit when you became believers?" They answered him, "We have never even heard that there is a holy Spirit." He said, "How were you baptized?" They replied, "With the baptism of John." Paul then said, "John baptized with a baptism of repentance, telling the people to believe in the one who was to come after him, that is, in Jesus." When they heard this, they were baptized in the name of the Lord Jesus. And when Paul laid [his] hands on them, the holy Spirit came upon them, and they spoke in tongues and prophesied. Altogether there were about twelve men. (Acts 19:1-7)

Peter said to them, "Repent and be baptized, every one of you, in the name of Jesus Christ for the forgiveness of your sins; and you will receive the gift of the holy Spirit." (Acts 2:38)

"We are witnesses of these things, as is the holy Spirit that God has given to those who obey him." [Peter is speaking] (Acts 5:32)

Now when the apostles in Jerusalem heard that Samaria had accepted the word of God, they sent them Peter and John, who went down and prayed for them, that they might receive the holy Spirit, for it had not yet fallen upon any of them; they had only been baptized in the name of the Lord Jesus. Then they laid hands on them and they received the holy Spirit.

When Simon saw that the Spirit was conferred by the laying on of the apostles' hands, he offered them money and said, "Give me this power too, so that anyone upon whom I lay my hands may receive the holy Spirit." But Peter said to him, "May your money perish with you, because you thought that you could buy the gift of God with money. You have no share or lot in this matter, for your heart is not upright before God. Repent of this wickedness of yours and pray to the Lord that, if possible, your intention may be forgiven. For I see that you are filled with bitter gall and are in the bonds of iniquity." Simon said in reply, "Pray for me to the Lord, that nothing of what you have said may come upon me." So when they had testified and proclaimed the word of the Lord, they returned to Jerusalem and preached the good news to many Samaritan villages. (Acts 8:14-25)

"As I [Peter] began to speak, the holy Spirit fell upon them as it had upon us at the beginning, and I remembered the word of the Lord, how he had said, 'John baptized with water but you will be baptized with the holy Spirit.' " (Acts 11:15-16)

And God, who knows the heart, bore witness by granting them the holy Spirit just as he did us. (Acts 15:8)

You may get the impression from this section that the Spirit did not exist or was not available before Jesus. This is not the case (§ 5.3.6).

5.3.2 Is Within

The Holy Spirit is a gift that is received from the inside. People who have the Holy Spirit are filled with him. To be filled with the Holy Spirit, is to be a man, or woman, of God.

But the angel said to him, "Do not be afraid, Zechariah, because your prayer has been heard. Your wife Elizabeth will bear you a son, and you shall name him John. And you will have joy and gladness, and many will rejoice at his birth, for he will be great in the sight of [the] Lord. He will drink neither wine nor strong drink. He will be filled with the holy Spirit even from his mother's womb, and he will turn many of the children of Israel to the Lord their God." (Lk 1:13-16)

The proposal was acceptable to the whole community, so they chose Stephen, a man filled with faith and the holy Spirit, also Philip, Prochorus, Nicanor, Timon, Parmenas, and Nicholas of Antioch, a convert to Judaism. (Acts 6:5)

"You stiff-necked people, uncircumcised in heart and ears, you always oppose the holy Spirit; you are just like your ancestors." [Stephen is speaking] ...

When they heard this, they were infuriated, and they ground their teeth at him. But he, filled with the holy Spirit, looked up intently to heaven and saw the glory of God and Jesus standing at the right hand of God. (Acts 7:51, 54-55)

When he arrived and saw the grace of God, he rejoiced and encouraged them all to remain faithful to the Lord in firmness of heart, for he [Barnabas] was a good man, filled with the holy Spirit and faith. (Acts 11:23-24)

The disciples were filled with joy and the holy Spirit. (Acts 13:52)

5.3.3 Gives Life

The Holy Spirit fills us with life. He is the source of life, both spiritual and physical. Know that the Greek and Hebrew words for Spirit can be used to mean wind, breath, or life. To have breath is to have life. To have the breath of God is to have the life of God within you.

"It is the spirit that gives life, while the flesh is of no avail. The words I [Jesus] have spoken to you are spirit and life." (Jn 6:63)

Jesus answered, "Amen, amen, I say to you, no one can enter the kingdom of God without being born of water and Spirit. What is born of flesh is flesh and what is born of spirit is spirit. Do not be amazed that I told you, 'You must be born from above.' The wind blows where it wills, and you can hear the sound it makes, but you don't know where it comes from or where it goes; so it is with everyone who is born of the Spirit." (Jn 3:5-8)

Now this is how the birth of Jesus Christ came about. When his mother Mary was betrothed to Joseph, but before they lived together, she was found with child through the holy Spirit. Joseph her husband, since he was a righteous man, yet unwilling to expose her to shame, decided to divorce her quietly. Such was his intention when, behold, the angel of the Lord appeared to him in a dream and said, "Joseph, son of David, do not be afraid to take Mary your wife into your home. For it is through the holy Spirit that this child has been conceived in her. She will bear a son and you are to name him Jesus, because he will save his people from their sins." (Mt 1:18-21)

But Mary said to the angel, "How can this be, since I have no relations with a man?" And the angel said to her in reply, "The holy Spirit will come upon you, and the power of the Most High will overshadow you. Therefore the child to be born will be called holy, the Son of God." (Lk 1:34-35)

5.3.4 Personhood

The Spirit is a person and not some sort of force of nature or divine energy. Jesus speaks of the Spirit, as recorded in the Gospel of John.

"And I [Jesus] will ask the Father, and he will give you another Advocate to be with you always, the Spirit of truth, which the world cannot accept, because it neither sees nor knows it. But you know it, because it remains with you, and will be in you." (Jn 14:16-17 There are similar passages in Jn 15:26, 14:26, 16:7-15)

The Spirit also leads, speaks, inspires, and teaches, which are the actions that persons can do, but things cannot. He does this from within. That is, when he speaks, he speaks through humans or directly to humans. When he leads, he leads people to take certain actions. The Spirit communicates with us directly. This is like prayer, but it is the Spirit speaking to us, rather than the other way around. I will list some examples:

As Jesus was teaching in the temple area he said, "How do the scribes claim that the Messiah is the son of David? David himself, inspired by the holy Spirit, said:
   'The Lord said to my lord,
    "Sit at my right hand
      until I place your enemies under your feet." '

David himself calls him 'lord'; so how is he his son?" [The] great crowd heard this with delight. (Mk 12:35-37; parallels in Mt 22:41-45; Lk 20:41-44)

Then Jesus was led by the Spirit into the desert to be tempted by the devil. (Mt 4:1; parallel in Mk 1:12-13)

During those days Peter stood up in the midst of the brothers (there was group of about one hundred and twenty persons in the one place). He said, "My brothers, the scripture had to be fulfilled which the holy Spirit spoke beforehand through the mouth of David, concerning Judas, who was the guide for those who arrested Jesus." (Acts 1:15-16)

"It is the decision of the holy Spirit and of us not to place on you any burden beyond these necessities, namely, to abstain from meat sacrificed to idols, from blood, from meats of strangled animals and from unlawful marriage. If you keep free of these, you will be doing what is right. Farewell." [In a letter from the apostles to Antioch] (Acts 15:28-29)

They traveled through the Phrygian and Galatian territory because they had been prevented by the holy Spirit from preaching the message in the province of Asia. When they came to Mysia, they tried to go on into Bithynia, but the Spirit of Jesus did not allow them, so they crossed through Mysia and came down to Troas. (Acts 16:6-8)

"Keep watch over yourselves and over the whole flock of which the holy Spirit has appointed you overseers, in which you tend the church of God that he acquired with his own blood." [Paul is speaking] (Acts 20:28)

As Peter was pondering the vision, the Spirit said [to him], "There are three men here looking for you. So get up, go downstairs, and accompany them without hesitation, because I have sent them." (Acts 10:19-20)

While they were worshiping the Lord and fasting, the holy Spirit said, "Set apart for me Barnabas and Saul for work to which I have called them." (Acts 13:2)

5.3.5 Guide to Truth

The Holy Spirit is the guide to truth. The Holy Spirit both grants us knowledge of the truth and empowers us to tell the truth to others.

"But I [Jesus] tell you the truth, it is better for you that I go. For if I do not go, the Advocate will not come to you. But if I go, I will send him to you. And when he comes he will convict the world in regard to sin and righteousness and condemnation: sin, because they do not believe in me; righteousness, because I am going to the Father and you will no longer see me; condemnation, because the ruler of this world has been condemned.

"I have much more to tell you, but you cannot bear it now. But when he comes, the Spirit of truth, he will guide you to all truth. He will not speak on his own, but he will speak what he hears, and will declare to you the things that are coming. He will glorify me, because he will take from what is mine and declare it to you. Everything that the Father has is mine; for this reason I told you that he will take from what is mine and declare it to you." (Jn 16:12-15)

"The Advocate, the holy Spirit that the Father will send in my name – he will teach you everything and remind you of all that I [Jesus] told you." (Jn 14:26)

"When they hand you over, do not worry about how you are to speak or what you are to say. You will be given at that moment what you are to say. For it will not be you who speak but the Spirit of your Father speaking through you." (Mt 10:19-20; parallels in Mk 13:11; Lk 12:11-12)

Then Zechariah his father, filled with the holy Spirit, prophesied. (Lk 1:67)

Now there was a man in Jerusalem whose name was Simeon. This man was righteous and devout, awaiting the consolation of Israel, and the holy Spirit was upon him. It had been revealed to him by the holy Spirit that he should not see death before he had seen the Messiah of the Lord. He came in the Spirit into the temple; and when the parents brought in the child Jesus to perform the custom of the law in regard to him, he took him into his arms and blessed God. (Lk 2:25-28)

Then Peter, filled with the holy Spirit, answered them, ... (Acts 4:8)

As Peter was pondering the vision, the Spirit said [to him], "There are three men here looking for you. So get up, go downstairs, and accompany them without hesitation, because I have sent them." (Acts 10:19-20)

But Saul, also known as Paul, filled with the holy Spirit, looked intently at him and said, "You son of the devil, you enemy of all that is right, full of every sort of deceit and fraud. Will you not stop twisting the straight paths of [the] Lord? Even now the hand of the Lord is upon you. You will be blind, and unable to see the sun for a time." Immediately a dark mist fell upon him, and he went about seeking people to lead him by the hand. (Acts 13:9-11)

5.3.6 Spoke Through the Prophets

You may get the impression from the section on the gift of the Holy Spirit (§ 5.3.1), that the Holy Spirit did not exist or was not available before he came upon the apostles. This is not true. The Holy Spirit has been acting in the world since Old Testament times, even though it was not as transparent. The strongest difference is that the Old Testament does not explicitly assert the personhood of the Spirit, and his distinct personhood from God the Father. The additional revelation of the New Testament allowed the church fathers to look back on the Old Testament and realize what had been missed before. There is no reason to believe that the Holy Spirit, as a person, sprang into being around the time of Christ, just because his nature became apparent to us then. Specifically, we know that the Spirit fills us (§ 5.3.2) and leads us (§ 5.3.5) to the truth. This is the best description of what happened to the prophets in the Old Testament. They were filled with the Spirit of God, who compelled them to proclaim truth. Below are some passages that support this.

> "You stiff-necked people, uncircumcised in heart and ears, you always oppose the holy Spirit; you are just like your ancestors. Which of the prophets did your ancestors not persecute? They put to death those who foretold the coming of the righteous one, whose betrayers and murderers you have now become. You received the law as transmitted by angels, but you did not observe it." [Stephen is speaking] (Acts 7:51-53)

Here, by opposing the prophets, the ancestors have opposed the Holy Spirit, which indicates that the Holy Spirit was in the prophets.

> "This is what was spoken through the prophet Joel:
>   'It will come to pass in the last days, God says,
>   that I will pour out a portion of my spirit
>   upon all flesh.
>   Your sons and your daughters shall prophesy,
>   your young men shall see visions,
>   your old men shall dream dreams.
>   Indeed, upon my servants and my handmaids
>   I will pour out a portion of my spirit in those days,
>   and they shall prophesy.' "
> [From Peter's speech at Pentecost.] (Acts 2:16-18; from Joel 3:1-2)

Joel is an Old Testament prophet. It is clear from the rest of Acts that when someone is spoken through, it is the Holy Spirit that is really the one doing the talking.

> "My brothers, the scripture had to be fulfilled which the holy Spirit spoke beforehand through the mouth of David, concerning Judas, who was the guide for those who arrested Jesus." [Peter is speaking] (Acts 1:16; referring to Ps 41:10; Lk 22:47)

> The spirit of the LORD shall rest upon him:
>   a spirit of wisdom and of understanding,
> A spirit of counsel and of strength,
>   a spirit of knowledge and of fear of the LORD,

and his delight shall be the fear of the LORD.
(Is 11:2-3)

The spirit of the Lord GOD is upon me,
    because the LORD has anointed me;
He has sent me to bring glad tidings to the lowly,
    to heal the brokenhearted,
To proclaim liberty to the captives
    and release to the prisoners.
    [The prophet Isaiah is speaking.] (Is 61:1; quoted by Jesus in Lk
    4:18)

But they rebelled, and grieved
    his holy spirit;
So he turned on them like an enemy
    and fought against them.
(Is 63:10)

Then the spirit of the LORD fell upon me, and he told me to say:
Thus says the LORD: This is the way you talk, house of Israel,
and what you are plotting I well know. [The prophet Ezekiel is
speaking] (Ez 11:5)

5.3.7 Divinity

It is apparent from the above sections that the Holy Spirit is
very special. He is a gift of God, lives within us, gives us life,
guides us to the truth, and is a person. He is not a person of
flesh and blood, but a person of spirit. Now, we have to decide
what sort of spiritual person he is. It is possible, because he
lives within us, that he is in some way our soul? This does not
make sense, because he is a person. Your soul is part of you. It
does not have a separate personality. Your soul does not lead
and teach you, it *is* you.

Is the Holy Spirit an angel? It becomes apparent on a careful
reading that this cannot be the case. The Holy Spirit has many
attributes that could only belong to God, not an angel. The
Spirit has divine knowledge. He knows all truth. He is not just

smart and knowledgeable, but all knowing, like only God can be.

> "But I tell you the truth, it is better for you that I go. For if I do not go, the Advocate will not come to you. But if I go, I will send him to you. And when he comes he will convict the world in regard to sin and righteousness and condemnation: sin, because they do not believe in me; righteousness, because I am going to the Father and you will no longer see me; condemnation, because the ruler of this world has been condemned.
>
> I have much more to tell you, but you cannot bear it now. But when he comes, the Spirit of truth, he will guide you to all truth. He will not speak on his own, but he will speak what he hears, and will declare to you the things that are coming. He will glorify me, because he will take from what is mine and declare it to you. Everything that the Father has is mine; for this reason I told you that he will take from what is mine and declare it to you." (Jn 16:7-15)

The Spirit gives life. None but God can give life. Others, such as human parents and angels only assist life. The fundamental source of life is God.

> Now this is how the birth of Jesus Christ came about. When his mother Mary was betrothed to Joseph, but before they lived together, she was found with child through the holy Spirit. Joseph her husband, since he was a righteous man, yet unwilling to expose her to shame, decided to divorce her quietly. Such was his intention when, behold, the angel of the Lord appeared to him in a dream and said, "Joseph, son of David, do not be afraid to take Mary your wife into your home. For it is through the holy Spirit that this child has been conceived in her. She will bear a son and you are to name him Jesus, because he will save his people from their sins." (Mt 1:18-21)
>
> Jesus answered, "Amen, amen, I say to you, no one can enter the kingdom of God without being born of water and Spirit. What is born of flesh is flesh and what is born of spirit is spirit. Do not be amazed that I told you, 'You must be born from above.' The wind blows where it wills, and you can hear the sound it makes,

but you don't know where it comes from or where it goes; so it is
with everyone who is born of the Spirit." (Jn 3:5-8)

Finally, there are some specific passages that indicate the
divinity of the Spirit, by placing him on an equal footing with
God the Father and God the Son.

> After Jesus was baptized, he came up from the water and behold,
> the heavens were opened [for him], and he saw the Spirit of God
> descending like a dove [and] coming upon him. And a voice came
> from the heavens, saying, "This is my beloved Son, with whom I
> am well pleased." (Mt 3:16-17; parallels in Mk 1:10-11; Lk 3:21-22)

> John testified further, saying, "I saw the Spirit come down like a
> dove from the sky and remain upon him. I did not know him, but
> the one who sent me to baptize with water told me, 'On whomever
> you see the Spirit come down and remain, he is the one who will
> baptize with the holy Spirit.' Now I have seen and testified that he
> is the Son of God." (Jn 1:32-34)

> Then Jesus approached and said to them, "All power in heaven and
> on earth has been given to me. Go, therefore, and make disciples
> of all nations, baptizing them in the name of the Father, and of
> the Son, and of the holy Spirit, teaching them to observe all that
> I have commanded you. And behold, I am with you always, until
> the end of the age." (Mt 28:18-20)

Because the Holy Spirit is a divine person, we should realize
that the relationship between the Holy Spirit and the other two
divine persons is eternal, using the same arguments that we
used for the Son's pre-existence (§ 5.1.6). This is supported in
scripture by the Holy Spirit's presence in the form of a mighty
wind at the beginning of creation (Gn 1:2), where we should
recall (§ 5.3.3) that the Holy Spirit is frequently represented in
scripture by breath or wind. What is the nature of this divine
relationship? We see from the conception and baptism of Jesus
(above) that the Father's love is given to the Son through the
Spirit. In this way, the Spirit proceeds from the Father to the
Son. Because the Son loves the Father in return, the Spirit also

proceeds from the Son back to the Father. The relationship between the Father and the Spirit forms one unified procession of mutual love. Note that proceed, when used in theology, refers explicitly to relationships between the three persons in God.

The issue of whether the Spirit proceeds from the Father and the Son or just from the Father is an old point of disagreement between the Roman Catholic and the Eastern Orthodox churches, so more support is necessary. The Spirit is not merely of the Father (Mt 10:20; Jn 15:26; 1 Cor 2:11), but also the Son (Gal 4:6; Acts 16:7; Rom 8:9; Phil 1:19). The Spirit is not only given by the Father, but by the Son (§ 5.3.1). The Spirit's knowledge comes from the Son. "He [the Spirit] will glorify me [the Son] because he will take from what is mine and declare it to you" (Jn 16:14).

5.3.8 The Holy Spirit and You

The Holy Spirit is a gift of God to you, not just some long-dead prophets, or some far-off saints.

When you feel that you are not up to the task of living the faith, God will give you what you need, if you but ask and allow him to guide you. What you need is the Spirit, who will fill you from within, to make you strong and bring you home.

When you feel empty, ask for the Holy Spirit, and he will fill you.

When you lose sight of truth, ask for the Holy Spirit, and he will guide you.

When you are weak and afraid, ask for the Holy Spirit, and he will give you power.

It is commonly said that God is too distant, too other-worldly for us to be near him. He has shown us that this is not the case. He loves you so, and desires you so, that he fills you from the inside and gives you true life.

This is the last section to describe an aspect of the nature of the Holy Spirit. At this point, we have discovered that there are three divine persons: God the Father, God the Son, and God the Spirit. Why then, do Christians call themselves monotheists, that is, believers in only one God? This requires us to understand The Trinity.

5.4 The Nature of the Trinity

We have learned that there are three divine and distinct persons, Father, Son, and Spirit. Scripture in general, and Jesus in particular, are explicit that God is one (Deut 6:4; 1 Kin 8:60; Is 42:8; Mk 12:29-32; Jn 17:3; 1 Cor 8:4-6; Gal 3:20; 1 Tim 2:5; Jam 2:19). How is this possible? It is analogous to the way that a family can be one, yet many. In a family, the husband is the lover, the wife is the beloved, and the children are the consummation (completion) of the love. Each person is their own person, but through love, they are brought together as one unit. God is similar, but much, much more so. All human families have flaws, but God's love is perfect. The Father is the lover, the Son is the beloved, and the Spirit is the consummation. God has three persons, but only one essence, one substance. Through the Trinity, we can reach a better understanding of our knowledge that God is Love (1 Jn 4:8). God's love exists within God, and is entirely self-supporting.

In addition, each person in the Trinity welcomes us into God's love. God the Father is around us sustaining all that is. God the Son is beside us as a man. God the Spirit is within us showing us the way. In these ways and through revelation, God welcomes us into God's love to a depth much beyond what would be possible without God's assistance.

CHAPTER 6:
Conclusions

6.1 The Foundations of Christian Knowledge

Let us look back at where we have been, so that we may discuss the foundations of Christian knowledge.

6.1.1 Natural Philosophy (Reason)

We can learn about God through natural philosophy (§ 3). We are able to learn about the greatness of God (§ 3.5) in all ways, including love (§ 3.7). We are able to understand that the law of love applies to us (§ 3.11). However, we lose many things when using only philosophy to learn about God. We don't learn about the Father (§ 5.2), Son (§ 5.1), and Holy Spirit (§ 5.3). We don't learn about the Incarnation (§ 5.1.6) and how Jesus is the interface (§ 5.1.8) between us and God. Even though we can learn about the love of God, philosophy does not show us the love of God expressed. For these things and many others, we need scripture.

6.1.2 Scripture (Revelation)

We have learned much about God from scripture, much more than we ever can learn from philosophy; so by example, we have learned that scripture is necessary to understand as much as possible about God. However, how do we know that scripture itself is reliable? It does appear on textual analysis to be the work of honest, careful men, who were writing about historical events (§ 4.2). Realize though, that in order to defend the authenticity of the work, we must also know who wrote it and when (§ 4.1) to verify that they were close enough to the actual events to know what they were talking about. For this, we rely on tradition.

6.1.3 Tradition

Tradition, taken narrowly, is a theological term which means the deposit of faith preserved by the Church that is not contained in scripture. It is not a tradition like painting eggs at Easter is a tradition. It is tradition in the sense that we remember who wrote the New Testament because of the information that the church fathers left us. Who wrote the New Testament is a key part of tradition, but from tradition we also get teachings such as the perpetual virginity of Mary. Since we use tradition to defend the authenticity of the New Testament, we implicitly assert that we can use tradition to defend the perpetual virginity of Mary. Reason, scripture, and tradition all have a difficulty, though. How do we know that we understand any of them correctly? If you have spent any time arguing the truth of Christianity with others, you have learned that the same passage can have wildly different interpretations by different people. In many cases, both people in the argument are well meaning, believing Christians; yet their differences of opinion lead to a dramatically different understanding of God. Things get even worse when discussing philosophy. It is not that difficult to find two philosophers with deeply held beliefs that are exactly opposite. To understand which person's beliefs corresponds to actual truth, we need some authority, some body which can resolve disputes. This authority is the Church.

6.1.4 Church (Magisterium)

We have come to the understanding that the Church is necessary to resolve differences of opinion regarding the content of Christian knowledge. However, which church? Let us look at what scripture and tradition tells us.

In the following verses, we see Jesus giving authority to humans. Authority is given to teach and cast out demons (or other evil).

> As he was walking by the Sea of Galilee, he saw two brothers, Simon who is called Peter, and his brother Andrew, casting a net into the sea; they were fishermen. He said to them, "Come after me, and I will make you fishers of men." (Mt 4:18-19) [All of the apostles were called in this way.]

> After this the Lord appointed seventy[-two] others whom he sent ahead of him in pairs to every town and place to visit. ... The seventy[-two] returned rejoicing, and said, "Lord, even the demons are subject to us because of your name." (Lk 10:1,17)

> Then Jesus approached and said to them, "All power in heaven and on earth has been given to me. Go, therefore, and make disciples of all nations, baptizing them in the name of the Father, and of the Son, and of the holy Spirit, teaching them to observe all that I have commanded you. And behold, I am with you always, until the end of the age." (Mt 28:18-20)

> And when he had said this, he breathed on them and said to them, "Receive the holy Spirit. Whose sins you forgive are forgiven them, and whose sins you retain are retained." (Jn 20:22-23; Mt 18:18 is similar).

In the next two verses, we see Jesus giving special authority to Peter. Peter is the rock, upon which Jesus will build his Church.

> He [Jesus] said to them, "But who do you say that I am?" Simon Peter said in reply, "You are the Messiah, the Son of the living God." Jesus said to him in reply, "Blessed are you, Simon son of Jonah. For flesh and blood has not revealed this to you, but my

heavenly Father. And so I say to you, you are Peter, and upon this rock I will build my church, and the gates of the netherworld shall not prevail against it. I will give you the keys to the kingdom of heaven. Whatever you bind on earth shall be bound in heaven; and whatever you loose on earth shall be loosed in heaven." (Mt 16:15-19)

When they had finished breakfast, Jesus said to Simon Peter, "Simon, son of John, do you love me more than these?" He said to him, "Yes, Lord, you know that I love you." He said to him, "Feed my lambs." He then said to him a second time, "Simon, son of John, do you love me?" He said to him, "Yes, Lord, you know that I love you." He said to him, "Tend my sheep." He said to him the third time, "Simon, son of John, do you love me?" Peter was distressed that he had said to him a third time, "Do you love me?" and he said to him, "Lord, you know everything; you know that I love you." Jesus said to him, "Feed my sheep." (Jn 21:15-17)

We also learn that Peter and the other apostles are not like other Earthly leaders. Even though they have power, power is not their primary purpose. Service is their primary purpose.

Then an argument broke out among them about which of them should be regarded as the greatest. He [Jesus] said to them, "The kings of the Gentiles lord it over them and those in authority over them are addressed as 'Benefactors'; but among you it shall not be so. Rather, let the greatest among you be as the youngest, and the leader as the servant. For who is greater: the one seated at the table or the one who serves? Is it not the one seated at the table? I am among you as the one who serves. It is you who have stood by me in my trials; and I confer a kingdom on you, just as my Father has conferred one on me, that you may eat and drink at my table in my kingdom; and you will sit on thrones judging the twelve tribes of Israel.

"Simon, Simon, behold Satan has demanded to sift all of you like wheat, but I have prayed that your own faith may not fail; and once you have turned back, you must strengthen your brothers." (Lk 22:24-32)

As we proceed forward in the New Testament, we see the apostles taking the authority that Jesus gave to them and granting it to others. In Acts 1:15-26, the apostles, led by Peter, selected (with God's direction) a replacement for the traitor Judas. In Acts 6:1-7, the apostles appoint assistants to help with the work of the Church. The apostles consecrate the new assistants by praying and laying on of hands, which is how deacons and priests are ordained to this day. In Acts 13:1-3, we see authority is given, with the direction of the Holy Spirit, to Paul (also called Saul) and Barnabas by the laying on of hands. This was done even though earlier Paul was called directly by Jesus in a vision (Acts 9:1-9, 1 Cor 15:8). Later, Paul writes to Timothy as a friend and superior in 1 and 2 Timothy. Paul speaks of the duties that Timothy was granted by the laying on of hands (1 Tim 4:14; 2 Tim 1:6) and Timothy's explicit duties as a bishop (1 Tim 3:1-13, 5:22; 2 Tim 4:1-6), including the selection of new bishops. In this way, we see the apostolic succession well under way in the New Testament.

After the period of the New Testament, we have the period of the early church. During this time, we have the writings of the church fathers. These fathers consistently defended the authority of Rome in general and the bishop of Rome (the pope) specifically. To cite a few of the many examples:

> Therefore shall you [Hermas] write two little books and send one to Clement [Bishop of Rome] and one to Grapte. Clement shall then send it to the cities abroad, because that is his duty. (*The Shepherd of Hermas* 1.2.4 ca. A.D. 80)

> You [the church at Rome] have envied no one, but others you have taught. I desire only that what you have enjoined in your instructions may remain in force. (*Ignatius's Letter to the Romans*, 3.1, ca. A.D. 110)

> Today we have observed the Lord's holy day, in which we have read your [Pope Soter's] letter. Whenever we do read it, we shall be able to profit thereby, as also we do when we read the earlier letter

written to us by Clement (Dionysius's *Letter to Pope Soter*, preserved in Eusebius's *Church History*, 4.23.11, ca. A.D. 170).

> But since it would be too long to enumerate in such a volume as this the succession of all the churches, we shall confound all those who, in whatever manner, whether through self-satisfaction or vainglory, or through blindness and wicked opinion, assemble other than where it is proper, by pointing out here the successions of the bishops of the greatest and most ancient church known to all, founded and organized at Rome by the two most glorious apostles, Peter and Paul, that church which has the tradition and the faith which comes down to us after having been announced to men by the apostles. With that church, because of its superior origin, all the churches must agree, that is, all the faithful in the whole world, and it is in her that the faithful everywhere have maintained the apostolic tradition. *(*Irenaeus's *Against Heresies* 3.3.2 ca. A.D. 189)

We see then that the authority was transferred from Jesus to Peter (and the other apostles) to the future popes (and the future bishops) in a smooth process. We then realize that the church that Jesus founded still exists today. It is the Catholic Church, which is led by the pope. Contrary to standard Protestant belief, there was no period when there was no authority in the Church. The church that the Protestants imagine to have restored has no historical basis.

Eastern Orthodox Christians, who broke off from Rome in the great Schism[20] (officially in A.D. 1054, unofficially the separation took many centuries), typically believe that the pope has a role of honor, but not one of authority. This is more reasonable than the Protestant view, but it is not consistent with the above evidence, especially the evidence from tradition.

Realize that as there must be a final authority on truth in the world (the Church), there must also be a final authority on truth

---

20 The relationship between Eastern Orthodox and the Roman Catholic churches is better than it has been in a long time, and with prayer and the assistance of God, we look forward to the reuniting of our family. See "Common Declaration of Pope John Paul II and The Ecumenical Patriarch Bartholomew I of Constantinople."

in the Church (the pope). To give each bishop equal and final authority would lead to no authority. This problem is realized to various degrees in both Protestant and Eastern Orthodox churches. Throughout history, there have always been bishops (or independent theologians) who bent or broke doctrine and had to be reined in by the pope.

However, how do we know that the Church has been faithful to its mission? Just because it was given a mission by Jesus does not mean that it has been true to it. In this matter, as in all matters, the Church relies upon God.

6.1.5 God

Jesus did not come only for the benefit of 1st century Jews. Jesus came for the benefit of the whole world, for all time (Mt 28:18-20, Is 59:21). If the Church failed to teach the message of Jesus correctly, a substantial part of God's efforts would be nullified. God will not allow the corruption of God's efforts, and therefore will not allow the corruption of God's message. If corruption is allowed to begin, it would only grow with time. More specifically, the Holy Spirit, as the guide to truth (§ 5.3.5), prevents the Church from making any error which weakens or distorts Jesus's message.

Which parts of Jesus's message are important, understood, and certain? The Church labels these as dogmas. Dogmas are those teachings which the Church asserts, by the power of the Holy Spirit, are infallibly true.

6.1.6 Infallibility

Infallibility is one of the most misunderstood teachings of Catholicism. Many opponents of Catholic Christianity do not try very hard to understand it properly because it is easier to contradict a false teaching than a true one. The official, summarized teaching is available in *The Catechism of the Catholic Church*, § 874-896. What must be understood is that the infallibility teaching is very restrictive. The pope is infallible when teaching *ex cathedra* (from the chair), or by the authority of the office of St. Peter on issues of faith and morals. The teaching must be declared to be binding to the whole Church, typically in an encyclical (church-wide letter). The pope is not infallible in his everyday life, when speaking as a private theologian, or when guiding a subset of the church. Even though the letter may be long, the infallible part typically consists of only a few sentences. Future popes are not free to contradict the content of the infallible statements of previous popes, though they may restate them using different language. Teachings that are understood to be true by the whole Church are often not declared as binding by the pope until a heresy (false teaching) appears that requires the pope to act against it. Most commonly, the true teaching is accepted by all for centuries before the heresy develops. Infallible teachings can also be declared as the result of an ecumenical (church-wide) council. These declarations are typically argued about and written by bishops, but a given declaration is not infallible unless the pope lends his infallible authority to that declaration.

As explained above, the rules for determining which statements are infallible are very strict. This leads to a tendency among liberal theologians to attempt to downgrade to a fallible statement any teaching with which they disagree. This tendency must be resisted. What must be realized is that you will never be in a dangerous state by following the teachings of the Church, but it is very easy to enter a dangerous state by contradicting the teachings of the Church. You would be advised to error on the side of caution when picking which teachings are only doctrines (teachings) and not dogmas (infallible truths). Erring on the side of caution typically means doing a fairly exhaustive search of Church teachings, past and present, and determining whether or not the requirements for infallibility have been met. If the requirements for infallibility have not been met, you must still look to see whether or not there has been widespread agreement in the Church throughout its history. The Church as a whole is continually guided by the Holy Spirit, even before the pope (with or without the assistance of the bishops) infallibly expresses that faith in definitive teachings.

This is not to say that the Church (or the pope) does not make mistakes. Different people put forth different ideas about what mistakes the Church has made; but we all agree that the Church has made mistakes, some of them severe. What this states is that when the Church claims to be infallible, it is; and when it does not claim to be infallible, it is not. In addition, if we study these mistakes in detail, we realize that they always come down to imprudent or unjust moral behavior of its members or leaders rather than mistakes in definitive teaching on faith and morals.

Fundamentals of Catholic Dogma, by Ludwig Ott, is a good source for understanding which teachings on faith are dogmas, and which are not. Each section is labeled with its grade of theological certainty. The labels are defined in the introduction (§ 8). In general, only the appropriately marked headings are considered infallible, not Ott's explanatory text. Note that there are also dogmas that are supported as much by tradition as by scripture (such as the perpetual virginity of Mary) and dogmas that are founded as much in reason as in scripture (such as the Trinity). Even though we reached an understanding of dogma by realizing that God would not allow the corruption of scripture, dogmas are also legitimate when they require tradition or reason. If the Church could declare any falsity as dogma, all teachings of the church would be rendered invalid. We do not have the freedom to pick and choose among the dogmas based upon their foundation. I have not found a good source that lists the moral dogmas. I believe this is because until the present day, most Christians agreed on what is good moral behavior and what is not, so there has not been as much need for the pope to make declarations.

The Catechism of the Catholic Church gives a comprehensive summary of the teachings of the Church, both faith and morals, but does not organize them by level of certainty. As stated above, though, you will never be in a dangerous state by following the Catechism, but you can easily enter a dangerous state by going against various bits of it. As John Paul II wrote in his introduction to the Catechism, it is a "sure norm for the teaching of the faith."

For the most part, the Catechism does not defend the teachings of the Church, it merely states them. If you are a Protestant, and have the usual Protestant objections to Catholicism (in addition to authority, which is covered above), I recommend that you look at Catholic Answers (http://www.catholic.com/library.asp), *Born Fundamentalist, Born Again Catholic*, by David B. Currie, and *Catholic Christianity*, by Peter Kreeft. I find that the most common difficulty when debating Protestants in that they state the teachings of the Church incorrectly, and then argue against that false teaching. After using these sources, you may not agree with the Catholic Church, but at least you will know what it actually teaches.

6.1.7 Inerrancy

Using similar arguments to § 6.1.5, we also understand that the Holy Spirit inspires and guides the writing, canonization, and preservation of scripture and prevents scripture from falling into error. We can now make a stronger and more accurate statement about the reliability of scripture than we made earlier (§ 4.2.3):

> The inspired books teach the truth. "Since therefore all that the inspired authors or sacred writers affirm should be regarded as affirmed by the Holy Spirit, we must acknowledge that the books of scripture firmly, faithfully, and without error teach that truth which God, for the sake of our salvation, wished to see confided to the Sacred scriptures." (*Catechism of the Catholic Church* § 107 following "Dei Verbum" § 11)

There are three key points here, each of which is frequently misunderstood. The first point is that scripture is inerrant because of the *active will of God*. In the end, it is only through the Holy Spirit's guidance that we can be assured that nothing vital has been left out or corrupted and that everything that is in scripture belongs. The second point is that scripture is inerrant *with respect to our salvation*. This is what is vital, and as such has the Holy Spirit's protection. Historical and scientific details are not necessarily correct, and must be evaluated using techniques from outside theology with an understanding that each human author writes from his own knowledge, world-view, and literary style. The third point is that *all* of scripture is without error with respect to salvation. In many cases, a single passage can have both a historical and a salvific meaning, or both a scientific and a salvific meaning. In some cases, such as the crucifixion and resurrection, a historical fact is vital to our salvation. Therefore, it is incorrect to say that parts of scripture are divine and parts of scripture are human, and we should only pay attention to the divine parts and throw away the rest. All of scripture is both divine and human and scripture should be read as a unified whole.

Finally, note that though scripture itself is inerrant as described, individual interpreters such as you or I are not. In order to have confidence in our interpretations, we must rely upon the wisdom of the Church (§ 6.1.4).

6.1.8 Mystery

Even though we have learned much about God, we have not learned all there is to know about God. Aside from the matter of my limited knowledge compared to that of the Church, we have no evidence that God has told us everything. Even if God did tell us everything, it is doubtful that we could understand it. Our minds and experiences are limited, while God's are infinite. Practical faith requires an acceptance of mystery: that there is more about God, infinitely more, than we will ever understand. We do not need to despair, however, for there is more than enough information for us to know the love of God and to properly live our lives as Christians.

6.2 Living as a Christian

Throughout this book, I have been focused primarily outward, towards God. This is as it should be. However, there has been a subtext: what the faith means for you. We learned that the Father will forgive you when you repent (§ 5.2.6), the Son will redeem you (§ 5.1.8), and the Spirit will guide you where you need to be (§ 5.3.5). We learned that acting with God, rather than merely being a list of rules and restrictions, is the only way to be fully free (§ 3.11).

This is all well and good, but I speak very little about what you must actually do to be a good Christian. That is the topic for some other book. Much more than that, it is a topic that must be lived, rather than read about. In order to have a guide for this life, it is necessary to join a community of like-minded persons. The Catholic Church, guided by the Spirit, is the correct community (§ 6.1.4). The community picks you up when you are down and corrects you when you are in error. It provides love and companionship on the long road ahead. With only your own power, you are not strong enough to be free of evil. With God's power and the Church's embrace, you are. "For human beings this is impossible, but for God all things are possible" (Mt 19:26).

About The Author

I (Matthew Grivich) received a B.S. in physics from Santa Clara University, and an M.S. and a Ph.D. in physics from UC Santa Cruz. Around the time I was completing my physics masters, I switched to a neuroscience project, so my Ph.D. is as much in neuroscience as it is in physics. I am currently working as a scientific programmer at the University of California in beautiful San Diego. This work primarily consists of developing software applications to assist in the study of neuroscience. My background allows me to see theological topics from a different perspective than is common. For philosophical questions, I am able to base my arguments in correct and current science. For scriptural questions, I demand a degree of rigor and structure that is rare in works of this type.

In addition to my formal education, I have a lifelong avocation to philosophy and theology. I was born into a Catholic household, but I absorbed the instinctive atheism of the wider culture at a young age. I have also always been a natural skeptic. That is, I error on the side of disbelief on most topics, both natural and supernatural. I demand rigorous arguments and strict structure before I believe anything. As time passed (about thirty years) I thought about God, read others' thoughts about God, starting writing this book, and eventually came to the understanding that the Catholic Christian faith is fundamentally rational. During the course of my journey, I have gone from atheist to strong agnostic to weak agnostic to deist to Christian to Catholic Christian. Even though I never stopped attending church, it is difficult to say that I was always a true believer. Now, I am back where I started, but sure that I made the correct decision. I recorded this journey in book form for three reasons: The first is so that if my work has real value to others, they will have access to it. The second is to keep me honest. I have to make the arguments good enough so that other people will accept them. Finally, there is nothing quite like trying to explain something to the world to motivate you to really understand it yourself.

First and foremost, I relied upon God in the writing of this book. I would also like to thank Bernadeane Carr, Br. Brain Coe, and Ann Grivich for detailed readings with significant insights and corrections. I would also like to thank Joe Morse and Eric Morse for their support and comments regarding the publishing process. In addition, I received assistance (in some cases unintentional) with various details from Jim Grivich, Chris Scott, Phillip Beaver, Joshua Emmanual Layton-Wood, Blair Reynolds, Ingrid van Welie, and Sam Maghsoodloo. Finally, I could never have produced a book such as this without substantial written sources, which I have referenced throughout the book.

Feedback is a critical part of the learning and writing process, and I encourage you to contact me with comments, questions, objections and corrections, whether they be slight or significant.

Matthew I. Grivich
mgrivich@systematicchristianity.org